Cambridge Elements

Elements in the Global Middle Ages
edited by
Geraldine Heng
University of Texas at Austin
Susan Noakes
University of Minnesota Twin Cities

THE GLOBAL MIDDLE AGES

An Introduction

Geraldine Heng
University of Texas at Austin

T0312049

CAMBRIDGE
UNIVERSITY PRESS

CAMBRIDGE
UNIVERSITY PRESS

University Printing House, Cambridge CB2 8BS, United Kingdom

One Liberty Plaza, 20th Floor, New York, NY 10006, USA

477 Williamstown Road, Port Melbourne, VIC 3207, Australia

314–321, 3rd Floor, Plot 3, Splendor Forum, Jasola District Centre, New Delhi – 110025, India

103 Penang Road, #05–06/07, Visioncrest Commercial, Singapore 238467

Cambridge University Press is part of the University of Cambridge.

It furthers the University's mission by disseminating knowledge in the pursuit of education, learning, and research at the highest international levels of excellence.

www.cambridge.org
Information on this title: www.cambridge.org/9781009161169
DOI: 10.1017/9781009161176

© Geraldine Heng 2021

First published 2021

A catalogue record for this publication is available from the British Library.

ISBN 978-1-009-16116-9 Paperback
ISSN 2632-3427 (online)
ISSN 2632-3419 (print)

The Global Middle Ages

An Introduction

Elements in the Global Middle Ages

DOI: 10.1017/9781009161176
First published online: November 2021

Geraldine Heng
University of Texas at Austin

Author for correspondence: Geraldine Heng, heng@austin.utexas.edu

Abstract: *The Global Middle Ages: An Introduction* discusses how, when, and why a "global Middle Ages" was conceptualized; explains and considers the terms that are deployed in studying, teaching, and researching a Global Middle Ages; and critically reflects on the issues that arise in the establishment of this relatively new field of academic endeavor. *An Introduction* surveys the considerable gains to be had in developing a critical early global studies, and introduces the collaborative work of the Cambridge Elements series in the Global Middle Ages.

Keywords: globalization, globalism, Global Middle Ages, world-systems, the global

ISBNs: 9781009161169 (PB), 9781009161176 (OC)
ISSNs: 2632-3427 (online), 2632-3419 (print)

Contents

1 The Introductory Elements in the Global Middle Ages Series

> The planetarity of which I have been speaking . . . is perhaps best imagined from the precapitalist cultures of the planet.
>
> Gayatri Chakravorty Spivak, *Death of a Discipline*

This is the first of two introductory Elements written by the editors of the Cambridge University Press series, Elements in the Global Middle Ages. This first introductory Element, *The Global Middle Ages: An Introduction*, is authored by Geraldine Heng, and accompanies the first-year rollout of titles in the Global Middle Ages series. The second introductory Element, *What Were the Middle Ages?*, authored by Susan Noakes, will accompany the second-year rollout of titles in the series.

The Global Middle Ages: An Introduction discusses how, when, and why a "global Middle Ages" was conceptualized; explains and considers the terms that are deployed in studying, teaching, and researching a Global Middle Ages; and critically reflects on the issues that arise in the establishment of this relatively new field of academic endeavor.

This concise study considers key issues of vocabulary, chronology, and themes central to the conceptualization and theorization of the global in pre-modernity; treats the relationship of global premodernity to global modernity; and surveys a variety of approaches to the global in earlier and emergent scholarship. It also compares our current moment's scholarship on the global with preceding as well as ongoing programmatic scholarship on world-systems theories, and the teaching of world history and world literature, in higher education today.

The second introductory Element, *What Were the Middle Ages?*, considers in detail the historiography of the period that, in common academic vocabulary, is conventionally called "the Middle Ages," by which is meant the *European* Middle Ages: a posited interregnum in the West between two glorified ages of empire and authority, Greco-Roman antiquity and its so-called Renaissance – an interregnum identified, named, and constructed by early-modern historiographers.

As we proceed, it will be apparent to readers that the discussions and arguments in both introductory Elements bring into focus the sustained import-ance of *critical* reflection and *critical* analysis.

Self-conscious reflection on the animating terms, methods, and objectives undergirding the study of global premodernity is essential as we move across a plethora of geographic vectors, temporalities, and disciplines. The editors of this Elements series thus view our promulgation of a "Global Middle Ages" as a call for a critical early global studies, and not as another academic enterprise by which unreflectively descriptive, summative, and taxonomic accounts of premodern worlds are adduced to compile a view of early globalism.

Organizationally, this Element is structured into sections, with headings that indicate the focus of each section. All section headings appear in the Contents page, for ease in locating and browsing a particular section. Readers are thus free to follow their interests, and consult whatever topics and sections interest them, in whatever order they wish, without having to hew to a narrative progression. Because each Cambridge Element allows for periodic updating, the series editors welcome questions and suggestions for future consideration and treatment.

2 All Good Things Have a Beginning: The When, How, and What of the "Global Middle Ages"

In 2003–4, one of us, Geraldine Heng, conceptualized and brought into being a collaborative teaching experiment in graduate education at the University of Texas at Austin. As the incoming Director of Medieval Studies at the time, Heng's remit from the then Dean of Liberal Arts was to revitalize medieval studies on campus. She also wanted to reimagine medieval studies anew, for the twenty-first century.[1]

There were exigent reasons to prompt a reconceptualization of how we should teach the deep past, one of which directly addressed the needs of the sociopolitical moment. In the aftermath of September 11, 2001, the West seemed to find itself in a temporal wrinkle in which the "Middle Ages" – always understood as European, and seen as an interval between classical antiquity and its revival in the early-modern period – was being invoked again by world leaders in the West and Islamist militants alike with respect to phenomena that seemed remarkably transportable from the past to the present.

The foremost leader of the Western world, George W. Bush, like the extra-state militant actors he condemned, was expatiating on crusades and crusaders in the context of international war. A model of empire as a form of governmentality in international affairs was approvingly reemerging in political theory. Dispositions of race practiced at airport security checkpoints, in the news media, and in public conversation suggested that *religion* – the magisterial discourse of the European Middle Ages, just as science is the magisterial discourse of the modern eras – was once more on the rise as a mechanism by which absolute and fundamental distinctions could be delivered to set apart

---

[1] Some of the thoughts and arguments in this Element adapt, revise, or reissue some of Heng's earlier published work on the subject of the Global Middle Ages. From the next paragraph onward, the first-person-singular pronoun is used by Heng.

human groups and populations by positing strategic essentialisms in a quasi-medieval racialization of religion.[2]

Even as the West was being haunted by premodern time, however, humanities departments teaching the past in institutions of higher learning continued to be calcified along disciplinary, national literature, national history, and area studies lines that atomized teaching; this made almost impossible a broad view across civilizations and systems that could deliver a multilayered, critical sense of the past in our time.

Nor did September 11 decenter the near-exclusive focus on Europe in literature and history departments in which the medieval period was taught. At best, courses like "Europe and Its Others" continued to be offered, and a new enthusiasm for teaching the crusades appeared. Area studies programs focusing on various territorial regions – the Middle East, South Asia, East Asia, and so forth – continued not to engage substantively with the teaching and study of other geographic zones and sociopolitical formations of the premodern world outside their specialized regions.

Augmenting the sense of urgency to deliver to students a multilayered view of the world in which the world's many vectors existed in intricate interrelationship was another, more quotidian imperative. I hoped that the experiment would incubate new habits of thinking and research among graduate students – foster a habit of reaching across cultures and methods, even as individual departments continued to ensure accreditation in local disciplinary training and knowledges – and that the process would, in time, produce a distinctive group identity for graduate students in a contracting national academic market.

Yet another urgent aim was to bring medieval studies, a field that was too often dismissed as concerned with largely obscure interests – with knowledges, it was thought, mainly interesting to academic antiquarians performing custodial functions for archives of little importance to anyone else – more visibly into conversation with other kinds of teaching and investigation in the twenty-first-century academy.

In 2003, an article by Kate Galbraith in the *Chronicle of Higher Education* had shown precisely what was at stake, by pointing to dangers that lay ahead for a field whose interests were thought to be unimportant to the rest of the academy, and unimportant to society at large. Galbraith reported *The Guardian*, quoting Charles Clarke, Great Britain's Secretary of Education at the time, declaring unctuously at University College, Worcester: "I don't mind

---

[2] On the neomedievalism and neoconservatism of the first decade of the twenty-first century, see Holsinger and Lampert. On race, see Heng, *The Invention of Race*.

there being some medievalists around for ornamental purposes, but there is no reason for the state to pay for them."

While medievalists in Great Britain were stung by Clarke's condescension and insult, they also seemed to flounder when trying to argue for their work's importance. A Cambridge University medievalist was quoted as falling back on an old academic vagueness, when she indignantly defended medievalists as "working on clarity and the pursuit of truth." Her lament that Clarke was "someone who doesn't understand what we do" touched on precisely the problem.[3]

Today, in 2021, the situation in Great Britain only appears to have worsened, as the University of Leicester reportedly prepares to replace its medieval curriculum with a decolonial curriculum prioritized by university administrators as urgently necessary in twenty-first-century England (Johnston, "Leicester University Considers Lessons in Diversity").

For the instructional faculty at the University of Texas, the opportunity to teach collaboratively was also attractive. Collaborative, interdisciplinary work in the humanities was the dream of many, but a dream that was often elusive. A classroom was a practical place for a beginning.[4]

To experiment with an alternative kind of learning, I assembled an instructional team of five faculty members from different departments, centers, and programs on campus, and two visiting faculty, to introduce to graduate students an interconnected, uncentered world, with points of viewing in the West and in Islamicate civilizations; trans-Saharan and North Africa; South Asia and India; the Eurasian continent; and China and East Asia. The "Global Middle Ages," a term I quickly coined in 2003 out of curricular and pedagogical necessity – mere expediency – was born.

It will hardly surprise any educator to hear that the classroom is an important incubator of new concepts and new projects. Faced with keen-eyed students eager to see what a different kind of pedagogy can deliver, the improvisations of instructors quickly devolve into strategies, and the strategies begin to plot pathways through intellectual thickets and carve a path into the future.

---

[3] In the United States, the ascent of white supremacists, nationalist extremists, and the alt-right – rabid racemongers who have deployed medieval symbols and images in support of their cause – means that medieval studies is less often seen today as an irrelevant discipline of interest mainly to antiquarians. See Kim, Lomuto, and Rambaran-Olm for examples of the use of the medieval past in ultraright violence.

[4] The senior administrators who supported the experiment in collaborative teaching – the Dean of the College of Liberal Arts and the Dean of the Graduate Division – saw that the course could function as a test case to identify obstacles to interdepartmental teaching, and, if such teaching proved feasible and desirable, identify solutions that could be entrenched as precedents for future collaborative instruction.

The instructional team decided to introduce cultures and vectors as interdependent but also discrete formations, without privileging any locations, and examined through a linked set of issues, questions, and themes. A decentered world would counter the ubiquity of Eurocentrism in pedagogy, and address the concerns of some areas studies scholars – such as those in Indian Ocean studies who objected to what they saw as the hegemony of Mediterranean studies (Grewal 187). To cultivate new contexts for studying a multilocational, uncentered past, the instructors did not descriptively survey, but critically assessed, the materials with which the class conjured.

In this way, the seminar sought not to replicate the world history surveys that were beginning to gain traction in the academy at the undergraduate level in lower-division courses of the early 2000s. Although world history surveys were, and remain, extremely important in delivering a broad perspective of the world, the instructors wanted greater depth of analysis for a graduate seminar, and to sustain an incrementally thickened sense, from week to week, of the complex interrelations that webbed the globe.

Fortunately, given that the fields of the instructional faculty included literary studies, social history, art history, material culture, religious studies, women's studies, the history of science and mathematics, and law and linguistics, interdisciplinarity was an inescapable condition of the teaching.

But rather than codify a priori how interdisciplinarity would function in the classroom, the instructional team of "Global Interconnections: Imagining the World 500–1500" worked through the pragmatics of the day-to-day pedagogical process, each member teaching from the disciplinary assumptions and practices most familiar to them, while reaching across to address what differed from their practices in the examples offered by their colleagues. The classroom was thus modeled as a kind of laboratory, with an open-ended process of trial, correction, and experimentation.

To the euphoria of all involved, the experiment proved a resounding success: Some students even voiced objections and regret that the course had to end at all. Everyone found the experiment exhilarating, and simply unlike any classroom experience we had known before.[5] Those involved included the then Dean of Liberal Arts, who had immediately volunteered to

---

[5] For detailed descriptions of the syllabus, the students, the problems that had to be overcome, and student conference papers and publications that resulted, as well as other features of the course, see Heng, "The Global Middle Ages" and Heng, "An Experiment in Collaborative Humanities." I first published an essay on the course in the *Medieval Academy Newsletter* (September 2004) at the invitation of the then Executive Director of the Medieval Academy of America, Richard K. Emmerson.

teach in the course when it was being designed[6] and two high-performing undergraduates who had special permission to enroll in a graduate class that met for six intense hours a week in the classroom and many more hours outside.

In its wake, as I lectured and published on how to conceptualize and teach a Global Middle Ages, I was asked, again and again: Why can't learning be more often like this? In response to that prompting, the coeditor of this Element series, Susan Noakes, then Director of the Center of Medieval Studies at the University of Minnesota Twin Cities, and I formally convened the Global Middle Ages Project (G-MAP) in 2007. Cohosting a workshop at the University of Minnesota, we invited premodernists and humanists from institutions of higher learning coast-to-coast in the United States, across several disciplines, to thrash out questions of terminology, definitions, timelines, and other issues.

Section 7 discusses the processes by which participants in that 2007 workshop arrived at the decision to retain the name, "the Global Middle Ages," which had been improvised out of expediency and necessity, despite the problematic nature of the name. The Global Middle Ages Project soon expanded into digital realms, as a way to forge a path to learning beyond the walls of a classroom. In 2008–9, a National Endowment for the Humanities (NEH) digital humanities grant, awarded to Illinois Computing in the Humanities, Arts, and Social Science (iCHASS) for G-MAP and two other projects, and coordinated by Kevin D. Franklin, iCHASS's Executive Director, brought groups of G-MAP's premodernists to three supercomputing centers – the National Center for Supercomputing Applications (NCSA), the San Diego Supercomputing Center (SDSC), and the Oak Ridge National Laboratory (ORNL) – to learn about high-performing computational methods and techniques. Subsequently, Susan Noakes convened a workshop at the University of Minnesota Twin Cities, on the digitizing of Istanbul/Constantinople, and a workshop in Tanzania, East Africa, on the digitizing of premodern Africa.

In 2011, Oxford historians in the United Kingdom convened a year-long series of workshops on the Global Middle Ages, inviting Noakes to the first of these, and following with a conference in 2012 and more workshops. Oxford's Centre for Global History soon launched a web page announcing the creation of

---

[6] A complicated "points" system accounting for faculty labor at the University of Texas in Austin required the Dean of Liberal Arts to approve staff releases to enable faculty to teach in this course. I was astonished (and greatly encouraged) when the then Dean of Liberal Arts, the Sanskritist Richard W. Lariviere (later provost at the University of Kansas, then president at the University of Oregon, and subsequently president of the Field Museum in Chicago until his retirement in August 2020), promptly volunteered to teach in the course himself. He proved a popular teacher, and a favorite of all the students in the seminar.

"a UK-based network of medievalists with interest in the global which has recently gained an AHRC [Arts and Humanities Research Council] network grant." In spring 2012, the University of Illinois at Urbana-Champaign convened a symposium entitled "The Medieval Globe: Communication, Connectivity, and Exchange," to which I was invited, a first step toward establishing a new academic journal, *The Medieval Globe*.

In 2012–13, Susan Noakes and I convened the Winton Seminar at the University of Minnesota, reshaping the original Texas course as a year-long graduate/postdoctoral/faculty seminar, with seventeen visiting and on-campus seminar leaders: "Early Globalities I: Eurasia and the Asia Pacific" in fall 2012 and "Early Globalities II: Africa, the Mediterranean, and the Atlantic" in spring 2013."

Two years later, with the aid of a Council on Library and Information Resources (CLIR) and Andrew W. Mellon Foundation grant, we launched a series of digital projects on www.globalmiddleages.org as a cybernetic classroom: a gateway to a kaleidoscope of learning that takes place outside university walls, and is open to all. The syllabus of the two-semester Winton Seminar can now be found on the Global Middle Ages platform at www .globalmiddleages.org/content/teaching.

A "Global Middle Ages" – transhumanities work that asks humanities scholars to step outside their discipline and area specialization to engage with other humanities scholars, social scientists, computer technologists, musicologists, archeologists, designers, and others to make sense of an interconnected past – now appears an idea whose time has arrived.

In the less than two decades since the term was coined, universities and colleges in the United States, United Kingdom, Europe, and Australia have begun undergraduate concentrations and graduate programs on a Global Middle Ages. Edinburgh University offers a Master's degree in art history on the Global Middle Ages, and Birmingham University offers a PhD degree on "Borders and Borderlands in the Global Middle Ages." In the United States, the universities of Pennsylvania, Minnesota, Connecticut, and Texas, the J. Paul Getty Museum, and Georgetown University, among other institutions, have had courses or programs, undergraduate and graduate, on a Global Middle Ages.

Three journals have emerged as the publications of record for this new field – *The Medieval Globe, Medieval Worlds,* and *The Journal of Medieval Worlds –* while an older journal, *Medieval Encounters,* which concentrated in the past primarily on interfaith encounters, and mostly in the Mediterranean, has retooled to incorporate a more global focus.

Academic symposia and conferences on the Global Middle Ages also abound. Among other venues, symposia and conferences on the Global

Middle Ages have been held at: the University of Illinois, Urbana-Champaign (2012), the Eastern European University (2014), the University of Wisconsin–Madison (2015), the Medieval Association of the Pacific at the University of California, Davis (2016), Indiana University (2016), the University of California, Los Angeles (2016, in art history), the J. Paul Getty Museum (2016, paired with a curated exhibition of global manuscripts that drew one million visitors), the University of Sydney (2016), and the University of Arizona (2014–17). Sydney University created The Global Middle Ages Research Group, a pan-Australian/New Zealand collaboration, in 2016.

As if to confer institutional blessing, the Medieval Academy of America, the flagship academic institution of medieval studies in North America, decided that the theme of its 2019 annual meeting in Philadelphia would be "The Global Turn." The Medieval Academy has also instituted a collaborative project with the National Humanities Center at the Research Triangle in the United States to produce a program of instruction and curricula for K-12 and college and university teachers on a Global Middle Ages. Since 2019, global-themed panels at conferences, symposia, and workshops have become increasingly common internationally.

Articles, special issues of journals, and edited anthologies on some aspect of a Global Middle Ages have also become increasingly common in the last decade, especially in the fields of history, art history, and literary-cultural studies, and are now too numerous to list. Publishers themselves began to commission texts: the Cambridge Elements series in the Global Middle Ages of which this introductory Element is a part, is one of these publishing initiatives.

Collaborative grants have been awarded by foundations to universities in the United States, the United Kingdom, and Australia to advance research, teaching, and digital humanities on a Global Middle Ages. In the United States, a half-million-dollar Mellon grant was awarded to the University of Minnesota Twin Cities, for courses and teaching on the global in premodern and early-modern studies; iCHASS was awarded a quarter-million-dollar NEH digital humanities grant for training and workshops at supercomputing centers; and the University of Texas was awarded a two-year CLIR/Mellon grant for a postdoctoral fellow to create the *MappaMundi* platform and digital projects at www.globalmiddleages.org. The University of California system awarded a generous collaborative grant to a consortium of historians at their Berkeley, Santa Barbara, and Davis campuses for research projects, workshops, and a new University of California Press journal, *The Journal of Medieval Worlds*. Oxford's Centre for Global History and Sydney University, have also been awarded grants for research and conferences on the Global Middle Ages.

These days, you can even buy flashcards online on the Global Middle Ages.

3 "An Idea Whose Time Has Come": Why the Global Turn in Premodern Studies Matters

The ease and rapidity with which the *idea* of the Global Middle Ages has spread, and the new-found enthusiasm for the global in early studies, suggests that teachers and scholars today are looking for something new to drive the transformation of early studies in the twenty-first-century academy. That enthusiasm for transformation in early global studies is not merely confined to premodernists: G-MAP's digital, teaching, and research projects on early globalism have been supported by modernists too, heralded by Cathy Davidson in *Academe* and by Gayatri Chakravorty Spivak in *PMLA* (166) as new ways to undertake teaching, collaborative work, and even reading in the twenty-first-century academy.

I like to think that this new-found enthusiasm for the global issues from the simple fact that the *gains* accruing from viewing the past globally are considerable. A global perspective of the deep past not only counters Eurocentrism, but can transform our very understanding of history and of time itself. It enables us to identify, for instance, not just a single Scientific and Industrial Revolution that occurred once, and exclusively in the West, but the recurrence of *multiple* scientific and industrial revolutions in the non-Western, nonmodern world.

For instance, the surviving artifacts of a ninth-century Arab ship recovered off the coast of the island of Belitung in Indonesia show us that Tang China mass-produced commercial ceramics on an industrial scale for the international export market nearly a thousand years before mass ceramic production in the West. When oceangoing transports were carrying 70,000 Chinese ceramic wares with features that were popular in the overseas market but not in China, and repeatedly crisscrossed the global maritime routes between the Persian Gulf and the port cities of ninth-century Tang China, we have material evidence of nonmodern industrialization on an impressively massive scale.[7]

Nor was Tang China's industrialization a singular event. The Sinologist Robert Hartwell's data shows us that the tonnage of coal burnt in Song China's iron and steel industries in the eleventh century was already "roughly 70% of the total amount of coal used by all metal workers in Great Britain at the beginning of the 18th century" – evidence, again, of nonmodern industrialization, this time in iron and steel manufactures, many centuries before the "Industrial Revolution" of the West (Hartwell, "A Cycle of Economic Change in Imperial China" 122; see also Hartwell, "A Revolution in the Chinese Iron and Coal Industries").

---

[7] This is a brief summary of long and complex arguments. For the long-form version, see Heng, "An Ordinary Ship."

The work of Joseph Needham and others, long known to historians of Chinese science, has for decades pointed to China's scientific, technological, and industrial innovations. However, because intergenerational transfers of knowledge tend to occur within academic silos that are sectioned off into departments, programs, and area studies, the "Scientific" and "Industrial" Revolutions remain "undead" – in the words of Mario Biagioli – both in the popular imagination and academic discourse today, as unique, exceptional, and singular phenomena. They continue to be taught as part of the foundational narratives of Western exceptionalism (see Hart, "Great Explanandum").[8]

By contrast, looking globally – and helped by the transdisciplinary impetus of a Global Middle Ages – we are afforded windows into deep time that open onto the existence of early, and multiple, industrial revolutions that can reshape our understanding of the past.[9] We become aware that what we are habituated to seeing as a singular and unique Industrial Revolution that only occurs once, and exclusively in the West, issues from a Eurocentric historiography that has reproduced, for generations, a grand foundationalist narrative of Western exceptionalism that is taught, and retaught, in academic silos of knowledge transmission.

Usefully, a transdisciplinary study of the global past in deep time erodes foundationalist narratives of a unique European genius, essence, climate, mathematical aptitude, scientific bent, or any other environmental, societal, genetic, or cognitive matrix guiding destiny in the "rise of the West" (a related grand narrative of the foundationalist kind).[10]

---

[8] Even linear algebra began in China, and moved westward, as the mathematician and Sinologist Roger Hart points out, undercutting claims of a unique Western genius for mathematics (see Hart, *Chinese Roots of Linear Algebra*).

[9] The poetic term, "deep time," is Wai Chee Dimock's, and adapted from the physical sciences.

[10] Rather than a unique European genius for science and technology, or a climate or environment that favored the West, history shows us that Western invasion, extraterritoriality, and colonialism are often the direct triggers for the so-called "rise of the West." The two-century history of the Crusades, for example, shows how, despite the eventual loss of all territories in Syria and Palestine, crusader colonization witnessed crucial transfers of agricultural, industrial, architectural, and engineering knowledges from the Levant to Europe, enabling the growth of European industries, agriculture, infrastructure, and artisanry. Europe's early colonial experiments thus shifted the economic calculus in favor of the Latin West, so that by the end of the medieval period – in an ironic reversal of their trade roles early in the Middle Ages – the East came to assume the erstwhile role of the West as exporter of raw materials over manufactures (see Heng, "Reinventing Race, Colonization, and Globalisms").

It is well documented that the dominance of Islamicate and Greek societies was eroded in export industries like sugar, textiles, and even fine, transparent glass. The economic consequences of the twelfth-century transfer of glassblowing technologies from Tyre to Venice can still be seen in the twenty-first century – it is Venice's Murano glass today, not Lebanese Tyrian glass, that is globally renowned and collected. As William Phillips wryly observes in his study of sugar production, while "the Crusades may have failed … in economic terms, they were successful, as the West wrested economic ascendancy from the East" (403).

4 Rethinking Time, Scientific and Industrial Revolutions, Modernity, and Premodernity

Nonmodern industrial revolutions like China's invite us to consider alternate, anti-essentialist ways of understanding history. Because premodern China's past attests to the difficulty of building on technological and scientific innovations in the context of repeated territorial invasion and political and social disruption, China's example restores an acknowledgment of the role of *historical contingency* – of randomness and chance – as operative factors in shaping civilizational history.

China's modernity-within-premodernity also guides an understanding of the plural nature of time – of how different temporalities can be enfolded and can coexist within a single historical moment. The example of China thus helps to make intelligible not only premodern worlds, but also societies around the globe *today*, which can seem modern, postmodern, and premodern all at once. Our view of time, of history, and of the relationship between modernity and premodernity is thus transformed when we see that multiple modernities have occurred in premodern time.

The historian Jack Goldstone has found *economic* modernities of both the Schumpetarian and the Smithian variety that have produced growth and change in societies and eras around the world. Tang China's mass-market industrial production of ceramics for a global export market on a scale that would not be seen in the West for another millennium, and Hartwell's data on the iron and steel industries of Song China evince an *industrial* modernity in early China.

For Europe itself, the work of Richard Britnell and Bruce Campbell, Joel Mokyr, D. S. L. Cardwell, Lynn White, and Jack Goldstone on the demographic growth, urbanization, and commercialization of the twelfth and thirteenth centuries suggests the recurrence of *demographic* and *commercial* modernities.[11] Alexander Woodside finds *bureaucratic* and *administrative* modernities in premodern China, Korea, and Vietnam.

Recurrent and multiple modernities whose *expression* varies across the globe and across time have thus been detected by a number of scholars. A global view across macrohistorical time urges an understanding that phenomena tagged "modern" or "premodern" can recur over the *longue durée*, each time with difference, each time not identically as before, in the multifarious vectors of the world. Accordingly, Susan Stanford Friedman suggests, with perfect logic, that we "abandon ... the notion of modernity as a *period*" altogether, and instead look at how modernity "articulate[s] differently on the global map of human

---

[11] See Goldstone (347) on urban populations, technology, and growth in medieval Europe, and his bibliography (380–389) for the work of Britnell and Campbell, Mokyr, Cardwell, and White.

history" (93; emphasis in the original). We come to understand that modernity itself is a repeating transhistorical phenomenon, with a footprint in different vectors of the world, moving at different rates of speed. Modernity is a modality that finds phenomenal expression, and not a chronological period.

5 Attending to Local, National, Regional, Global: The Politics of Intertwined, Interlocking Scales of Relation

Seeing the global in this way yields startling insights and recognitions, but the importance of a global perspective by no means shunts aside or obviates the continuing importance of studying the local and the national. For those of us who have been trained in particular national literatures, languages, and histories, a global view in fact invites a perspective of how national and global forces can interlock, as a country acts locally within its borders and internationally across the globe in shaping a new national and global identity for itself.

Iberianists can point to Spain's persecution and expulsion of Jews and Muslims – a moment of self-purification constitutive of the early Spanish nation – as that moment, also, when Spain's global-colonial ambitions arose and began to spread Spain's umbra across the world. As it forcibly emptied itself of people it saw as belonging elsewhere in the world, Spain, under the Catholic monarchs, also made its governance bloom elsewhere in the world. The spread of Spain's national boundaries outward in the form of Hispanized colonies around the globe – in the Americas, the Philippines – thus affirmed the forces of Spanish nationalism and Spanish imperialism–globalism as mutually constitutive and interlocking in the formation of Spain's national and global identities.

All this, and more, is visible in literature and history, when we look globally. The advancement of early global studies therefore does not mean the elision or the relegation to unimportance of the local, nor the end of studying national languages, literatures, and histories, including microhistories. In fact, to see how nationalism and colonialism–imperialism are interlinked and mutually constitutive dynamics requires training and viewing at *both* local *and* global scales.

In the same way, the study of globalism by no means obviates the continuing and necessary work of regional studies – Mediterranean studies, Indian Ocean studies, Atlantic studies, etc.[12] – but merely positions a reminder that, for the world's inhabitants, every place is the center of the world and that for multifarious scholars worldwide there is no single region of supreme historical significance and priority above all others.

---

[12] Important contributions to regional studies in premodernity include the highly successful Mediterranean Seminar (now being rebranded to develop a more global emphasis), the North of Byzantium project, and various Global Asia and Indian Ocean initiatives, among others.

Of considerable urgency today, for those of us trained as Euromedievalists, is that highlighting the overlap between the local, the regional, and the global undercuts the fantasy that an earlier Europe was the opposite of Europe now, a continent with global populations from all around the world.

The study of premodern transglobal slavery and human trafficking, transnational migrations, global commerce, and international wars foregrounds archives that enable us to bear witness to an early Europe that already contained people from everywhere – Jews, Arabs, Turks, "Gypsies," Africans, Indians, Mongols, steppe peoples, and others – and refuses the fiction that a singular, homogenous, communally unified, Caucasian ethnoracial population once existed in a Europe that was still Latin Christendom.[13]

Beyond traditional archives of historical data, contemporary bioarcheological investigation also supports globalist perspectives of race, genetic mixing, and racial hybridity among the populations of medieval Europe. Archeologists are discovering that even in the far northwestern corner of the world, in premodern England, the cemeteries of East Smithfield in London yield genomic and biomorphic evidence that, nestled in the graves of the interred during the Plague years of 1348–50, were the remains of people of nonwhite ancestry – primarily Black African, Asian, and intermixed ethnoracials – who constituted some 29 percent of the bodies interred there (Redfern and Hefner 106). Bioarcheological evidence, it would seem, shows nonwhite Londoners carrying ethnoracial DNA from other parts of the globe to be far more common than was suspected by earlier generations of precritical scholarship on medieval race.[14]

The notion that an all "White" Europe existed as a historical *fact* – and not as an idea manufactured by centuries of assiduous identity construction – is thus exposed as the fantasy of contemporary politics and political factions in the West today. The study of the global past in deep time can thus speak productively to the racial politics of the contemporary European and Western now, and make "present political conversations more historically responsible," as Amrita Dhar puts it, so "that we can use the past" to build "just futures."

In the twenty-first century of rabid Trump-style politics and politicians, Brexit, and the insurgencies of alt-right and white supremacist movements in the United States, the United Kingdom, and Europe, the study of a Global

---

[13] See, for example, Heng, *Invention of Race*, chapter 3, "A Man for All Seasons: Saladin, and How the West Made New Races; or, Slavery, Sexual Mixing, and Slave Dynasties."

[14] The DNA of Norse maritime raiders commonly known as *Vikings* has also been reported to be more diverse than formerly considered. A multi-authored genetic study by Ashot Margaryan et al. that sequenced the DNA of 442 men, women, and children from burial sites found evidence of genetic influence from Southern Europe and Asia in a period from 750 CE to 1050 CE, as reported in the journal *Nature* (Margaryan et al.).

Middle Ages can thus be an act of intellectual allegiance to ethical responsibility.[15]

Acknowledging the presence of the world within Europe, while uncentering Europe's presence in the world, has other important consequences. In a forum on *The Invention of Race in the European Middle Ages* in the *Cambridge Journal of Postcolonial Literary Inquiry*, Cord Whitaker, an African American medievalist, reports that he is repeatedly asked where Black people were in premodernity:

> The perception that Black people have no history – or at least no history from before chattel slavery in the Americas – is common in the western world. It has prompted otherwise well-educated professionals to ask me, incredulously, 'Where *were* the Black people in the Middle Ages?'.

It would seem that the hegemony of Europe, buttressed by widespread ignorance of premodern Africa, has made it possible for the "otherwise well-educated" to ask a question of this kind without embarrassment. One important aim of these Cambridge Elements and an instituted perspective of the global is to make it impossible for *anyone* to ask this question.

Also of considerable importance is the fact that a critical early global studies works not only to decenter Eurocentrism and Eurocentric apparatuses of knowledge, but also to undermine ethnocentric and hegemonic paradigms that configure knowledge *in other locations of the world*. For Sinologist art historians, the global turn in art history has supported a shift away from dominant nationalist modes of Chinese historiography that have constrained what can said about Chinese art, and by whom, as well as what methods and approaches are deemed appropriate for the interpretation of Chinese art:

> In this respect, the broader implication of global art history is not merely the decentering of geographical focus from the West to elsewhere, where it has always been for some of us; rather, it is the simultaneous decentering of dominant narratives and categories of Western scholarship *and* (in many cases) the dissolution of the Sinocentric traditionalist paradigms that have distorted Chinese historiography and art history (Cheng 26, emphasis in the original).

---

[15] The Medievalists of Color, an anti-racist scholarly advocacy collective, has documented the rise of white supremacy and the alt-right in the United States in a series of blog posts, conference panels, workshops, and talks (see https://medievalistsofcolor.com). Graduate students are also playing their part in combating neoconservative extremism: At Columbia University, funded by a small Mellon grant, medievalist graduate students in the Art History and History departments assembled a Medievalist Toolkit to furnish the media with information and resources to counter the falsehoods and distortions retailed by the alt-right in public discourse about the premodern past.

Summarizing "the historical framework that still dominates the story of premodern Chinese art" as a "rhetoric of Han superiority" that began with the May Fourth movement – a rhetoric that has been "consistently reaffirmed and calcified since the Communists took power" – Bonnie Cheng tells us that alternate, revisionist approaches to viewing Chinese art, culture, and history "continue to be resisted within China" today, so that promulgators of new approaches are accused of "fabricating a 'history of China from an imperialist standpoint'" (22–23).

"Historians outside China have argued convincingly that 'Han,' as an ethnic category, is a modern invention," yet the traditionalist–nationalist framework of scholarship on China continues to "identify the Han as simultaneously ancient and fundamentally impervious to change or contamination by other cultures" (Cheng 23; see also Mullaney et al.). But like the fantasy of an all-white, homogenous, Latin Christendom/early Europe, hegemonic historiographies of the Chinese kind also become vulnerable once a global perspective of interconnection, exchange, and transformation is introduced.

Even as China's traditionalist–nationalist framework of art interpretation continues to essentialize Han Chineseness and insist on the nonhybridity of Han art, Cheng optimistically observes that the very unpacking of the complex interactions and exchanges with multifarious cultures and artists that produced a Chinese art object in premodern time – scholarship that is occurring in global art historical studies today – counters Chinese ethnocentrism and essentialist notions of Han identity and superiority, and frees up new methodological approaches and interpretations.

Attention to the global significantly "allows for the recognition of the many pathways and paces of artistic exchange," but nonetheless "need not distract us from local conditions and particular contexts" (Cheng 28–29).

6 What *Is* Early Globalism? The World, the Globe, and the Planet, Part One

Implicit in the study of the global is thus an embedded perspective of the interconnecting relations and exchanges that occur across often large geographies of space. It is important to remember that the global is always "*an instituted perspective*," "a way of bringing into view the world" through "an approach to the comparative study of cultures" (Krishnan 1, emphasis added).[16]

---

[16] Sanjay Krishnan reminds us that "the global" doesn't simply have an empirical existence, but is in fact "an instituted perspective" that views the geophysical and empirical world in particular ways by examining its connective and comparative relations (1).

Accordingly, the study of *globalism* can differ from the study of *the world* in a number of ways.

Studying the world in world history courses, for instance, involves learning about a wide collection of places with individual cultures, histories, and societies, some of which may or may not be introduced in relation to the others. In literature departments, world literature courses bring together a miscellany of texts to represent the many cultures and localities of the world, to offer a snapshot of the world's literary creations in the form of best practices. Themes or genres may then be deployed to scaffold the smorgasbord of texts into organizational coherence.

The study of globalism, however, begins with, and foregrounds *interconnectivity*: in the first instance, the interconnectivity of lands around the world whose cultures, stories, religions, languages, art, goods, germs, plants, and technology were braided into relationship across distances that may have seemed vast, perhaps even almost unimaginable, in their time.[17]

Yet a focus on interconnectivity, whether of an artistic, commercial, linguistic, technological, religious, scientific, agricultural, political, martial, or epidemiological kind, also enables us to see that early globalism involves not just a concept of *space* – how geographical spaces and vectors were interlinked, say, by trade or commerce – but also that globalism exists as a *dynamic*: as forces pushing toward the formation of larger scales of relation.

Globalism can readily be seen at work, of course, when *Pax Mongolica* secured overland routes, and moved artisans and goods around the vast Eurasian continent from termini to emporia, so that an English king, Edward I, in a far northwestern island of the world could wear Chinese brocade as part of his coronation robes.

But globalism is also at work when a religion like Islam makes its way out of Arabia's Hijaz and moves eastward to South Asia, or westward to Africa, dynamically transforming local occupations and personal statuses, and reshaping rituals, politics, stories, and roles; or when Indic culture scatters across island Southeast Asia, spreading architectural styles, languages, mythologies, Buddhism, and Hinduism. That is to say, early globalism also exists as a dynamic: as forces that globalize.

Although this Element began with an epigraph by Gayatri Chakravorty Spivak on planetarity, it's necessary to acknowledge from the outset that in terms of spatiality, *the global* in premodernity is not the same thing as *the*

---

[17] The art historian Alicia Walker reiterates that "twentieth-century 'world' history ... focused on local histories in comparative terms, with only secondary attention paid to connections among regions," whereas, by contrast, "global history of the late twentieth and early twenty-first century foregrounds linkages among cultures" (183).

planetary, and a premodernist working on the global should not feel a requirement to address every place on the planet, nor feel a corollary obligation to establish the interconnectivity of each corner of the earth with every other corner of the earth.

The only way that *the global* in premodernity can be said to edge toward *the planetary* is in the sense of projective forces (religious, commercial, linguistic, etc.) that drive toward an unrealized horizon and involve a scale of ambition and entanglement exceeding what was achievable, if not imaginable, in their time. At most, in premodernity, we have a *drive* toward planetarity, the envisaging of which is not the same thing as its achievement.

In geospatial terms, actualized, planet-wide interconnectivity did not exist in premodernity. Although Europeans in the form of Greenlanders and Icelanders crossed the Atlantic Ocean to reach the North American continent circa 1000 during the Little Climatic Optimum (also known as the Medieval Warm Period, or the Medieval Climate Anomaly), they did not cross the Pacific Ocean to reach Austronesia. While Chinese imperial "treasure ships" helmed by the Yunnanese Muslim eunuch-admiral Zheng He crossed the South China Sea and Indian Ocean to reach Africa in the fifteenth century, they did not arrive in Austronesia, the Americas, or Antarctica.

Extraordinarily, DNA research in plant biology now seems to indicate that Polynesians may have traversed half the world to reach the South American continent circa 1000, but there are as yet no suggestions that the inhabitants of Oceania arrived in Siberia or Greenland. Concomitant genomic research argues, conversely, that Native South Americans may have reached the Pacific Islands in the twelfth and thirteenth centuries, but no claims currently exist that these South Americans also arrived in Siberia or Mongolia (Ioannidis et al.; Armitage).

Early globalism of the spatial kind is therefore by no means synonymous with an interknitted planetarity, nor with contemporary globalization's (admittedly uneven) webbing of the world today. Indeed, early globality is not tantamount to and should not be equated with twenty-first-century globalization either, a globalization that – at least in theory – knits together the inhabitants of all pockets of the planet in space–time today through contemporary technology (see Sections 9 and 10 for crucial distinctions between these concepts and terms, as well as the different historiographic and epistemological contexts in which the concepts and terms have arisen).

Usefully, the art historian Alicia Walker, citing a short blog essay by Joseph Nye, reiterates Nye's insight (in turn borrowed by Nye from James Clifford's cultural heuristic of "thick" and "thin") that premodern globalism necessarily manifested unevenly all over the world:

It must be acknowledged from the outset that the medieval world did not witness a truly global network, with all continents of the earth linked through economic, political, and cultural relations. Yet globalism need not require a total system; it can instead be productively understood as relative, manifesting in "thick" or "thin" and complete or partial degrees (Walker 183; see also Nye).

From all this, we can see that for the inhabitants of the premodern world, what constituted the global – and whether globalism existed as an operative force in daily life lived on the ground, or as a set of social relationships between regions, or as a port tax on a dhow's cargo from another hemisphere – necessarily differed from place to place, and according to someone's location on the globe. Early globalism took many forms for different peoples in the many localities of the globe, and manifested diversely, unevenly, and differentially from place to place.

7 What's in a Name? The European "Middle Ages," the "Global Middle Ages," and Premodern Time around the Globe

An understanding of what early globalism is, and what it is not – for instance, that globalism is not planetarity or globalization, and globalism can manifest in different ways, and to different degrees (thickly or thinly, partially or fully) in the many regions of the world – may be less difficult to arrive at than a way to *name* early globalism to the satisfaction of all.

What is at stake in a name? Edward Said pointed out decades ago (a length of time that seems like an eon, on a scholarly timescale) in his pathbreaking book, *Orientalism*, that the constitution of an object of knowledge and study *rapidly turns into the thing itself*. When you name a place *Egypt*, for instance, and add a description, that name and description then become the thing itself for you – in your mind and understanding, and in everyone else's. We do not distinguish an empirical Egypt that is separate from the Egypt we have as an object of knowledge – the Egypt we've named, described, studied, and think we know.

In post-Saidian eras, we might say, with Sanjay Krishnan, that naming the global matters, because "the global as a frame and an operation constitutes and produces the region it claims merely to describe" (1). How we name, and see, is a process that is *constitutive* and *generative*, and not a process that merely registers what is already "out there." As we see in the various sections of this Element, the stakes involved in a name, and in the naming process, can be considerable.

A number of issues were on the agenda for the participants of the formative 2007 planning workshop at the University of Minnesota. A wide array of questions and issues on globalism were discussed extensively and in depth.

Differences in disciplinary training; varied disciplinary assumptions and methods of viewing; the diverse and even rival forms of attention that different premodern objects of study demanded; even the very status of the objects of study themselves and their priority in the academy, or lack thereof, were hashed out and rehashed over a number of days during the workshop.[18]

From the beginning, however, all were conscious that the very name with which we were conjuring for our project, "the Global Middle Ages," was a problem.

The Euromedievalists among us were keenly aware that the use of the term the "Middle Ages," a construct fabricated by early-modern historiographers to name an interregnum between two glorified ages of empire identified by their putative supremacy in the West – Greco-Roman antiquity and its so-called Renaissance – relegated a thousand years of premodern time to ancillary status.

The very concept of a "Middle Ages" thus required critique of its ideological freight. For one of us – the coeditor of this Elements series, and codirector of the Global Middle Ages Project, Susan Noakes – this commonplace term, the "Middle Ages," could only be embraced under erasure, and accepted only contingently, as a contested Eurocentric construct with little or no epistemological bearing for the not-Europe cultures of the world, and perhaps with little bearing even for Europe itself.

For Euromedievalists unreflexively to export the "Middle Ages" to territories beyond Europe in naming chronologies in other zones of the world would thus inadvertently be a colonizing gesture by Euromedieval studies: the centrality of European time giving its name to asynchronous chronologies elsewhere, so that there is an Indian "Middle Ages," an African "Middle Ages," a Japanese "Middle Ages," etc.

Clearly, those of us who would embrace a Global Middle Ages need to acknowledge and respect the fact that the zones and cultures of the world are asynchronous, and follow different timelines of description, naming, change, development, recurrence, and transformation. Differential temporalities characterize the many zones of the world.

---

[18] One memorable exchange took place over a consideration of what premodern objects were worthy of our attention, and what approaches were needed for these objects. To the literature scholars and historians present, documentary materials were, of course, of prime importance, while art historians discussed a variety of plastic and visual art objects. Discussion by the archeologists at the symposium concentrated on beads and coins until one individual, Kairn Klieman, objected to this very traditional focus. What about rice, she demanded? Why not focus on the movement of rice around the world? Suddenly, the participants – who had been discussing how to read texts, images, coins, and beads – had to consider how to read a grain of rice. What forms of attention do we bring to a grain of rice, when discussing computational methods, close analysis, or anything else?

The pitfalls of exporting Europe's chronology and a European system of naming to the rest of the world are underscored by Emma J. Flatt in her essay on how to teach the histories, literatures, and cultures of South Asia, written for my Modern Language Association (MLA) anthology, *Teaching the Global Middle Ages*.

Patiently, Flatt shows us that the importation into South Asia of a Western model of periodicity imposed by British colonial masters, with their Eurocentric template of dividing time into "classical," "medieval," and "modern" periods, historically served the expediencies of British colonial–imperial rule; today it winds up colluding with Hindu nationalist interests that are busily relegating India's Muslims to secondary status as citizens:

> When the British began writing the history of India, they conceived of a tripartite schema, dividing India's pasts into ancient, medieval and modern. However, the specific historical periods to which these labels applied were determined on the basis of the religion which was judged to be in the ascendant: the ancient period mapping onto the "Hindu" period (judged to stretch from the earliest times to the Ghurid invasions of c.1192); the medieval period mapping on to the "Muslim" period (from 1192 to the British victory at the Battle of Plassey in 1757); and the modern period being identified, by the colonialists, self-declared bringers of "civilization" and "modernity," as the "British" period (1757–1947).

For British-ruled India, the "classical" period was characterized by "a timeless and unchanging" Hinduism, "with Sanskrit as the language of politics, religion and high culture"; the "medieval" period was the time when "an expansionist and aggressive Islam" brought foreignness to India, a characterization that willfully obscures, Flatt wryly observes, "the dynamism and far-reaching significance of Hindu-Muslim encounters in multiple domains of political, religious, social and cultural life." The onset of the modern period, ending the Islamicism of medieval time, began when British rulers brought civilized British principles to Indian shores, and ushered the fortunate subcontinent into the enlightened world-community of the British empire.

"Although scholars have been challenging this tripartite division of Indian time since at least the 1980s," Flatt reports, "it has remained surprisingly persistent in popular discourse." In fact, the renowned Indologist historian Romila Thapar, who has challenged the description of South Asian history as a tripartite chronology favoring "classical" and "Hindu" greatness before the fall into a contaminating "medieval," "Muslim" interregnum, has received death threats from Hindutva ideologues because of her critiques.

So what's at stake in the naming of a period? For a scholar under threat of death for contesting European hegemony in the naming of time around the world, more than we might suppose. Yet, even as Flatt highlights the problem of naming several centuries of Indian history and culture as "medieval," she recognizes the necessity of communicating with her readers in terminology of sufficient familiarity to them – so as not to risk an alienation that would put in jeopardy a volume of teaching essays aimed at offering help to encourage readers to find ways of incorporating the worlds of South Asia into their teaching, rather than discouraging that effort.

Accordingly, Flatt makes graceful concessions that point to why premodernists who are not Europeanists may nonetheless continue to use Eurocentric models for periodizing time: "On the other hand, re-aligning South Asian chronology with the accepted chronological breaks of Western history ... does present an interesting opportunity to reflect on continuities ... and an opportunity to examine linkages with the rest of the world."

Feeling the tug of contradictions, Flatt's scholarly compromise is revealing. First, she points to the political stakes of importing European terminology to name her subject area, the subcontinent of India, and makes us conscious of what is recommended, occluded, and sacrificed in that naming. Then, she nonetheless makes a decision to use terminology that is familiar to scholars working in Western literatures, histories, and languages, by pointing to what is gained in using a vocabulary that links her field to other fields, including Euromedieval studies.

In similar fashion, some scholars of other non-Western zones – of Africa, or Islamicate civilizations, or Japan, for instance – have also decided to conjure with terms like "the medieval" and "the Middle Ages" in identifying periods in the historiography of their zones. Their references to the "Islamic Middle Ages," "Jewish Middle Ages," "medieval Japan," (or even the "North American Middle Ages," as Tim Pauketat, one of the foremost archeologists of Cahokia and the Mississippi basin prefers it) can thus be seen *both* as the hegemonic ineluctability of European studies' dominance in the academy, *and* as efforts of goodwill on the part of non-Europeanists in accepting the utility of certain overarching heuristic paradigms across geographic zones.

These heuristic paradigms may bring attention to features and characteristics that suggest resemblance or analogy between varied zones and chronologies, and can act as bridges that allow for conversations between colleagues working in different disciplines and geographic zones when thinking about possible linkages across differences.

Needless to say, *situated terminology of this kind, issuing from within non-European studies, and attached by their scholarly proponents to their own zones and periods of study, carries a different valence from its attachment by Euromedievalists, willy-nilly, to chronologies and zones around the world.*

Scholars of non-European zones and regions may, like Emma Flatt, preface the imperfect choices open to them with a critical discussion that highlights the stakes involved in their decisions over terminology – or they may elide that discussion because the stakes seem clear and obvious to them. Indeed, a number of contributors to this Cambridge Elements series in the Global Middle Ages may simply elect Flatt's strategy, as they present their zone and field of study when authoring their own Elements.

Terms like the "Islamic Middle Ages," or "medieval India," can then be seen as crucial compromises that point to academic vocabulary's limitations, and to Euromedieval studies' hegemony in the academy, even as such terms enable and facilitate conversations across a broad spectrum of premodern studies.

Compromises of this kind, in naming and terminology, do not mean that we of the Global Middle Ages Project have not reflected critically on the naming of our own project, or have not made scrupulous and conscientious efforts to find alternative names for "the Global Middle Ages." At the 2007 workshop in Minnesota, several attempts were made to rename our collective endeavor, with other names being tried and considered.

"Global *Pre*modernity" seemed to some to retain attention too fixedly on modernity as the focal point of an implicitly linear temporality, and had the disadvantage of temporal vagueness. It was pointed out that "premodernity" could indicate the Bronze or the Iron Age, Biblical time, or Greco-Roman antiquity all the way through to the so-called Renaissance, which is still considered by some as a premodern era.

An inspired suggestion, by a graduate student, that we call "the Global Middle Ages Project" the "1001 Years Project" met with objections from a historian who thought the reference to *The Thousand and One Nights* lent an unfortunate aura of fantasy to the project. My own preferred term, "Early Globalities," was felt by the same historian colleague to signal too strongly the work of literature departments rather than history departments.

All attempts at naming the past thus pointed to the inescapability of the conceptually and politically freighted nature of the language we had to use in order to participate in academic discourse. In the end, to be able to speak at all among ourselves and to others, we agreed to continue the use of conventional terms, but also to continue to critique the terms and highlight their problematic nature.

In a sense, therefore, we were following in the footsteps of preceding academic movements: Poststructuralist critique of logocentrism and feminist critique of phallogocentrism did not work to produce alternate linguistic systems, but to critically highlight consciousness of the stakes involved in language use. I have thus reiterated, in lectures and publications, that ethical and epistemological responsibility to the emergent field of early global studies requires autocritique and continued awareness of the politically, epistemologically, and socioculturally freighted character of the animating terms, concepts, vocabularies, timelines, and methods we apply.[19]

Once we accept that time across the globe is asynchronous, and scholars of different regions and zones can describe the chronologies and historiographies of their areas in ways that do not find it necessary to link up with European time, nor with the temporalities of other, Western or non-Western, regions and zones, the sheer adventitiousness of fixed chronological parameters for the projects of the Global Middle Ages becomes readily apparent.

The conventional time parameters identified in the West for the "Middle Ages" – neatly adumbrated as 500–1500 CE – are little more than a heuristic fiction, of convenience mainly as a way to round off the jagged edges of history by placing fantasmatic borders around messy and sticky historical phenomena that do not hew to temporal confinement. The digital, research, and teaching initiatives of the Global Middle Ages Project have thus foregrounded or critiqued the hegemony of a Europe-based, factitious Roman-calendar periodization hedged at one end by the collapse of the Roman empire (neatly located as circa 500 CE), and at the other by the incipience of the early-modern era or so-called Renaissance in the West (neatly located as circa 1500 CE), and have rejected temporal rigidity in favor of a plethora of timelines around the world.

The Cambridge Elements series in the Global Middle Ages also hews to no rigid temporal parameters as universal markers, leaving it instead to subject specialists of the world's different geographic zones to instruct us, and readers, on how to think about temporality in their geospatial areas. Obviously, what scholars of China or India might designate as appropriate chronological parameters for their zones may differ from what scholars of Oceania and Pacifica might designate as appropriate for *theirs*. Indeed, even within an area of study, ways to mark the progression of time or narrate the historiography of a zone may be contested, volatile, and in process, depending on the state of academic discourse in the disciplinary field.

In the field of art history, Bonnie Cheng points out that within the study of Chinese art, "Jonathan Hay … has questioned our reliance on the political frame of dynastic time, and even the temporal unit of the century, as problematic markers for artistic practices that may not align with political or temporal shifts" (25 n. 42). Cheng even finds it necessary to begin by carefully denoting

---

[19] Gratifyingly, some contributions in recent edited volumes on the global (see, especially, Keene, and Normore) show attempts to reflect critically on the concepts, methods, and timelines we apply to the study of early globalism, and have prioritized critical reflection and discussion.

precisely what she means by "China," and how she applies descriptors of the region's time and China's history:

> I use "China" in this essay to designate the contemporary geographic terrain, recognizing that boundaries have shifted over its lengthy history. I refer to specific centuries when possible but use the term "premodern" for expedience, knowing that it asserts a problematic binary with modern. I acknowledge that the use of the term "medieval" with reference to China may evoke an imperfect temporal frame, but do so in the spirit of the stated aims of [the anthology in which Cheng's essay appears] (11 n. 1).

For the editors of this Cambridge Elements series, the lack of a satisfying alternative name for the *Global Middle Ages* as well as descriptors like *medieval* is most keenly felt when communicating with scholars who work in non-Western geographic zones – as, for example, when we formally introduce them to the work of the Cambridge Elements on early globalism. Potential contributors to the Elements series, reviewers of manuscripts, audiences at talks – all who are not Euromedievalists – often struggle when they hear the term "Global Middle Ages," because of what the "Middle Ages" signifies to them in academic and popular discourse.

Understandably, and to no surprise, many non-Europeanists are reluctant to apply the term *Global Middle Ages,* and its adjective, *global medieval,* to the historiography of their zones and prefer to eschew such naming altogether, given significant differences in their own timelines and the modes of periodization that have been established in their own, non-Eurocentric, disciplines. Because we need a shared vocabulary in order to talk, the use of conventional academic vocabulary exacts a price that we all continue to pay.

8 Why Periodization Still Matters: Acknowledging Epistemic Shifts and Differences across Time

Although a global perspective allows us to see the recurrence of multiple modernities around the world over macrohistorical time – undercutting the grand narratives and platitudes of foundational historiography in the West – we should not imagine that refusing the reduction of time into a calcified, fixed binary of premodern and modern periods means a renunciation of *all* forms of periodization.

The critical study of early globalities does not carry the objective of *ending* periodization as such, but rather urges the rethinking of old chronologies, chronotopes, and entrenched historiographies of temporality, so as to prompt a reconsideration of their investments and politics.[20] The salient question to ask, then, is not, "Is premodern time absolutely different from later periods?," but "What is at stake in saying that it is, and characterizing it thus-and-thus?" Or, conversely, not, "Is premodern time the same as later periods?," but "What do we lose when we say it is?" In fact, fidelity to the particulars of historical phenomena requires us to acknowledge the occurrence of epistemic shifts and differences across time, and also to bear witness to distinctions that characterize phenomena that recurred across the *longue durée*.

Periodization matters. One key example is the institution of slavery. Slavery as an institution in what we call the medieval period assumed a variety of forms and was an equal opportunity condition for *all* races and populations. The slavery endured by the Romani ("Gypsies") in Wallachia and Moldavia spanned centuries from the late-medieval well into the modern era, but Romani domestic and field slavery in southeastern Europe differed considerably from Egypt's Mamluk military slavery of the mid-thirteenth through mid-sixteenth centuries (Heng, *Invention of Race* chapter 7).

For the Mamluks – elite military dynasties comprising primarily Turkic and Circassian slave boys plucked from continental Eurasia and raised among other slave boys as professional warriors – the Sultan of Egypt and Syria could only be drawn from the ranks of former slaves. For the most powerful Islamic polity of the southern Mediterranean and Levant until the ascendancy of the Ottomans, the requirement of having once been a slave was thus an indispensable condition of eligibility for the highest office in the land (Heng, *Invention of Race* 138–150).

In parallel fashion, prized Caucasian female slaves in Islamic Spain or in the Levant could rise to become the revered mothers of caliphs, sultans, and emirs – or, in the case of the remarkable Shajar ad-Durr, to become, arguably, the only Mamluka in the three-century history of the Mamluk dynasties. In Dar al-Islam, extraordinary social mobility meant that being a slave could be an important first step to power, wealth, status, and authority – an avenue of upward mobility open, importantly, to women. (Heng, *Invention of Race* chapter 3). This is not the case for plantation slaves in the later American south.

Premodern slavery can thus be seen as distinct from early-modern and modern slavery, especially the chattel slavery of North America, and distinct also from the mutating forms of slavery (including child sex trafficking) that dog the twenty-first century. Caucasians and eastern and western "Europeans"

---

[20] The recognition that it's necessary to retain periodization in some form, for the reasons suggested in this section, while contesting current periodicities, does not evade the concomitant recognition that periodization as an exercise is a form of discipline marked by investments and interests.

were sold at slave markets alongside all other races throughout the period we call the Middle Ages, distinguishing medieval slavery from later, Africa-sourced chattel slave labor in the early-modern and modern periods.

Household slaves were common and typical in the premodern period; plantation and field slaves were statistically less attested.[21] Some enslaved persons had considerable autonomy and independence, and were entrusted with considerable responsibility by those who had purchased them. Amitav Ghosh's meticulous excavation of the particulars of an Indian slave in Mediterranean and Indian Ocean trade of the twelfth century demonstrates, for instance, how enslaved individuals could develop into trusted commercial agents acting on behalf of absent entrepreneurs.

The subject investigated by Ghosh was an enslaved man identified in archival documents only by the consonants "B-M-H," who was owned by the India trader Abraham ben Yiju in the mid-twelfth century. Ghosh's research suggests that this enslaved individual had probably been purchased in Malabar and was later entrusted with conducting business for his master in Egypt and across the Indian Ocean. Tracing the man's life through the mention of him in Cairo Genizah letters to Abraham ben Yiju from business contacts, Ghosh meticulously stitches together archival evidence to retrieve a figure from the past who was a key example of an enslaved individual functioning as a trusted business agent in Indian Ocean commerce, and who repeatedly supervised and accompanied cargoes of ships back and forth between the Mediterranean and the Indian subcontinent.[22]

Much attention has been lavished by literary critics, postcolonial studies scholars, and Euromedievalists on Ghosh's *In an Antique Land: History in the Guise of a Traveler's Tale*, but it is Ghosh's article in the journal *Subaltern Studies*, "The Slave of MS.H.6," that shows in detail how he extracts the circumstances of a Malabar slave's life from the anonymity of an 800-year-old global past and makes that life intelligible to modern readers. In the process, Ghosh learns that "slaves from western Europe were regularly traded in India and China" ("Slave of MS. H.6" 169) and he reiterates: "Slavery in [t]his era had none of the connotations that European capitalism was to give it after the sixteenth century. It was a common practice for merchants in [Abraham ben Yiju's] position to recruit slaves as business agents and apprentices" (Ghosh, "Slave MS. H.6" 170).

---

[21] Medieval slavery is a complex subject that has accrued an extensive body of scholarship. For some points of entry, see Verlinden, Constable, Phillips (*Slavery in Medieval and Early Modern Iberia; Slavery from Roman Times*), Epstein, Barker, and Heng (*Invention of Race* chapter 3).

[22] See Ghosh, "Slave of MS. H.6," and also Goitein and Friedman's introduction to letters addressed to Abraham Ben Yiju by his business associate, Khalaf b. Isaac (594–596).

Indeed, outside the lands of medieval Christendom, manumitted persons who were formerly enslaved might become generals, admirals, diplomats, and governors; historical archives around the globe are replete with documents attesting to the distinguished careers and lives of former slaves. Depending on time, place, religious confession, and political and economic conditions, slavery in the medieval period could mean abject, subaltern misery for an exploited population, or it could be a sine qua non condition for the highest offices in the land, or a variety of other possible situations in between.

The sheer variety of medieval slavery's conditions and opportunities thus attest to very specific differences within the medieval period, as well as between medieval and later periods in the phenomena that characterized the institution we call slavery. Continuities in some modalities of slavery across medieval and early-modern time, but also *dis*continuities between the racial slavery of these historical periods, remind us that in discussions of race, distinctions must be honored with the acknowledgement that periods can be marked off differentially by institutions and phenomena that can recur, but recur with varied manifestations, over the *longue durée*.

Africa-Mediterranean-Indian-Ocean commercial and cultural relations also witnessed a massive sea change from the medieval to the early-modern period, with the advent of European colonial expeditions along the maritime routes of the Afro-Asian world. The aftermath of Vasco Da Gama's arrival in India post-1498 saw the incremental conscription of the centuries-old Indian Ocean trade by the Portuguese (and later, the Spanish, Dutch, British, French, and others), and the weaponizing of commercial relations when Portuguese fire power and militarism ended the peaceful trade relations that had been sustained by peoples of different continents meeting to transact commerce in the Indian Ocean over many centuries of premodern time.

While militant European extraterritoriality in the Mediterranean may be seen to have occurred as early as the crusading eras of the eleventh century and afterward, it is the early-modern era that witnessed the onset of Europe's maritime empires on a global scale.

In the long history of imperialism, medieval colonization in the form of the Crusades had an important role to play in later European colonialism. Medieval Latin Christendom's crusading propaganda invoked *religion and God* as the authorizing discourse of its colonial enterprise, setting in motion a template of colonization indispensable to the later European colonial expeditions that would arrive around the world – not like ancient Rome and antique forms of empire, but like Latin Christendom – wielding *both* the Book *and* the sword to subjugate, civilize, and convert the so-called heathen populations of the world.

Invading lands; subjugating diverse populations; extracting resources; reconstituting whole economies; ruling over and experimeting with entire countries, regions, and subcontinents; "civilizing" populations by converting "heathens" to Christianity; and dominating the trade routes of the Indian Ocean and Asia with firepower: The early-modern era and, following that, the modern era, witnessed European imperialist aggression and the weaponizing of commercial relations in the oceans and seas of Asia on a scale that had no precedent in premodernity.[23]

This is a transformation that distinguishes medieval-era trade and commercial relations around the globe from the extractive, exploitative, and violent colonial relations that characterized early-modern- and modern-era commerce around the world in the wake of aggressive European imperialism. Early-modern European imperialism witnesses epistemic change of an order and on a scale that is altogether new, and must be recognized as such. In the history of empire-formation – in the scale, duration, and methods of Europe's extraterritorial colonial enterprises of aggression, extraction, and occupation – periodization also matters.

Like the transformed, militarized, and unequal trade relations that came to web the postmedieval world, art that functioned in the service of empire also found different modes of expression during the medieval and early-modern eras. Building on the work of Jean Devisse, Paul Kaplan, and Güde Suckale-Redlefsen, I have argued that the Black St. Maurice of Magdeburg Cathedral in east Germany – a sandstone statue of a sainted martyr who was the leader of the Theban legions under a persecutory imperial Rome – was suddenly depicted as a Black African, with iconographic Saharan features, because of the usefulness of that transformation to a thirteenth-century history of failed crusades, the ambitions of the Holy Roman Empire, and a dream of Christianity's militant and Pentecostal reach over the far corners of the earth in the thirteenth century (Heng, *Invention of Race* 222–242).

---

[23] This is not to say, of course, that premodern imperialism did not exist around the world. Beyond the well-known examples of Rome, and the Mongols, Geoff Wade discusses Chinese imperialism, one strain of which is spectacularly manifest in the shock-and-awe "treasure-ships" of the Ming imperial fleet commanded by the Muslim eunuch admiral Zheng He in the fifteenth century. Although Zheng He's naval expeditions are popularly assumed to be voyages of "exploration," Wade points to the Chinese fleet's colonial behavior in maritime Southeast Asia, where the fleet forcibly deposed local rulers, installed surrogates, and intervened muscularly to shape local and regional politics in the South China Sea and Indian Ocean (see also Shaoyun Yang's volume on premodern China's view of "barbarians" and premodern China's supremacism). But the *global scale* of the devastation wrought for *centuries* by Europe's maritime empires around the world, the effects of which continued to be felt even after the former imperial subjects freed themselves from their colonial yoke through decolonization, is of another order altogether.

For art that was serviceable to imperial ends in the early-modern era, Jessica Keating and Lia Markey point to two genres of painting – the still life and the landscape – whose development advanced in tandem with early-modern European empire:

> Dutch still life painting in the seventeenth century, which was extremely popular at the height of the Dutch trading empire, is a case in point. As Dutch ships brought more and more goods from Asia and the Americas, still lives became increasingly more lavish in content and complex in composition. Like the commodities around the world they pictured, still life paintings became commodities that were fervently bought up by individuals on all rungs of the social ladder. This entanglement of the artistic and the economic was also importantly political. Through their ubiquity, as Julie Hochstrasser has shown, still life paintings were one of several mechanisms that naturalized Dutch presence throughout the world. (212)

In the early-modern era, even as Dutch still lives delivered a form of art that functioned in the service of empire, we notice that such imperially serviceable art has, by this time, become *privatized* and has multiplied, hanging in individual private homes rather than being displayed for public viewing and communal veneration in the shared space of a cathedral.

Art of this kind still depicts and displays the exotic in service to empire, like the Black St. Maurice statue in Magdeburg, but unlike the communal veneration of a sainted figure, this *secularized* art also serves a double purpose, since "the prominence of exotica in Dutch homes and in Dutch painting was paradoxically seminal to the creation of a Dutch national identity" (Keating and Markey 212).[24] According to Keating and Markey, looking globally in the early-modern era reveals a dynamic of nationalism and a dynamic of imperialism–colonialism converging and interlocking in the genre of secular, privatized painting known as the Dutch still life.

That is to say, in the early-modern era the privatization of art on a wide scale ("fervently bought up by individuals on all rungs of the social ladder," as Keating and Markey put it) under demotic conditions – where the possession of art is not confined to royalty, nobility, ecclesiastics, or wealthy elites – in tandem with the widespread secularization of European art, signally points to important economic, sociological, and technological transformations that occurred between epistemic formations in due course of time.

---

[24] Images of the Black St. Maurice also multiplied in the medieval period; nearly 300 artifacts bearing the image of the Black Maurice have been counted by Güde Suckale-Redlefsen (16, 17, 158–285), Paul Kaplan (75), and Jean Devisse (270–271), spread across Germany, Scandinavia, the Czech Republic, Austria, and Poland. The images, nonetheless, all depict a sainted figure, and Maurice's sanctity continued as an important touchstone.

The socioeconomic, technological, and epistemic shifts taking place between the (European) medieval and the (European) early-modern become visible, and are announced, through altered conditions of ownership, medium, and functionality in the register of art and art objects. In tracking the altered conditions, Keating and Markey highlight the new phenomenon of artistic mass production (at last!) in Europe: "[T]he development of the woodcut and the engraving allowed for the mass production of images," so that along with the spread of printing in the West,

> This moment signalled both the rise of the artist as endowed with intellectual invention and the power of the printed image to disseminate not only the artist's imagery but also his name . . . engravings rose in prominence throughout the sixteenth century and became the central form of artistic production to disseminate style and subject matter across the globe . . . the prints designed by the Flemish artist Giovanni Stradano, who lived in Florence, made their way to Mexico and South America within a few years of their production in Antwerp. (211)

I suggested in my 2003 book, *Empire of Magic: Medieval Romance and the Politics of Cultural Fantasy,* that what has often been called "travel literature" in the medieval period – that is, literature that described what the faraway world was like to audiences back home in Latin Christendom, whether or not the authors of the literature actually traveled – constituted a way to make the world mobile, and to bring *souvenirs* to an audience in Europe. These souvenirs took the form of vignettes, anecdotes, and stories about exotic phenomena, foreign folks, curious flora and fauna, and sensational spectacles that would delight, horrify, and serve as enjoyable recreation for audiences at home (Heng, *Empire of Magic* chapter 5).

Literature of this kind, while claiming to relay information about the vast world at large, in fact *miniaturized* the vast world's lands, customs, peoples, and objects into thrilling and enjoyable, exotic particulars – collectible souvenirs for an audience in the West so that they might sample and possess the delights and terrors of the world without having to leave home. Medieval European travel literature – a literature of wonders and marvels, as scholars have duly noted – thus narrated the vastness of the world while simultaneously miniaturizing that world for audiences in Christendom, rendering the world's exotica collectible, in story form.

Medieval European travel literature, I urged, was therefore a precursor, in anecdotal-narrative form, of the wonder-boxes and cabinets of curiosity of the early-modern era, and, beyond that, a precursor of the modern museum. Exotica collected in anecdotes, vignettes, and stories that filled the travel narratives of the medieval period were replaced, in the early-modern period, by physical souvenirs and exotica that were collected to fill the wonder-boxes of the time, inhabiting cabinets of curiosity, and eventually, inhabiting the museums of the modern eras.

This is to state the obvious: that while *trajectories* of collecting have continued across deep historical time, *modalities* of collecting, and the *display* of collected exotica, may shift across epistemic formations and registers. In the twenty-first century, computational methods and digital media have again reshaped collecting and display, as some physical objects and exotica are now presented only in their virtual forms: materializing as online digital images, or via 3D immersive technology, or augmented reality environments, all of which may, or may not, be accompanied by digital storytelling (a postmodern counterpart to the medieval travel narrative).

Collections of the world's exotica – whether these assumed the form of vignettes, or physical objects in a box or cabinet, or appear in room after room of a building – when amassed and arranged to relay specific kinds of information about the world, in specific ways, are not innocent, as museum studies and museum theorists have shown so well. Museum studies has discussed the politics of museum collection, curation, and display extensively. A well-known twentieth-century example is James Clifford's "On Collecting and Culture" in his influential *The Predicament of Culture*. A recent twenty-first-century example is a coauthored essay by two medievalists of color, the art historian Andrea Myers Achi and the literary scholar Seeta Chaganti.

Clifford analyzes "'the art-culture system' through which . . . exotic objects have been contextualized and given value in the West" (215). Achi and Chaganti emphasize that the curation and display of "Medieval African Art" in particular requires "careful approaches to undoing the implicitly colonial elements of museum spaces, highlighting original contexts, and sharing understudied narratives" (76, 78). Achi and Chaganti go on to suggest creative curatorial practices – including ways to label, position, and group artifacts, and use space strategically – in order to challenge museumgoers to see relationships and meanings they might not otherwise see in museum displays (98–100).

Chaganti offers the recent "Caravans of Gold, Fragments in Time" exhibition at Northwestern University's Block Museum, curated by Kathleen Bickford Berzock, as an example of curatorial practices that consciously engage with the politics of curation in ethically responsible ways:

> Caravans of Gold . . . partnered with cultural and museum commissions in Nigeria, Mali, and Morocco. It experimented methodologically, drawing upon the techniques of "archeological imagination" to speculate from fragments, challenging traditional curatorial practices. It concerned itself with cultural heritage protection and migration. It intriguingly sets the stage for

interrogating museum projects, asking to what extent can established cultural and educational institutions fully participate in achieving politically and socially emancipatory aims.

But before new and ethically responsive ways to present the artifacts of the world were consciously researched and enacted, collections of the world's exotica – whether in the form of material objects, or vignettes in popular medieval travel literature – presented the world in Eurocentrically charged ways.

One example of a popular travel account that decisively shaped European views about what the world was like was the late-medieval *Mandeville's Travels* – whose blockbuster dispersion for centuries across the Latin West saw its translation into all the major European languages, and has left us with more than 300 surviving manuscripts today. This travel account, which shaped the particulars of the world to support the author's dream of a pan-Christianity that would transform the globe into an empire of the Christian faith – at the expense of Jews, Muslims, and peoples of other faiths – harnesses its collection of story-artifacts to a dream of dominion that would not be unfamiliar to the later colonial empires of Europe that also sought Christianized coloniality (Heng, *Invention of Race* 349–382).[25]

The early-modern era, Keating and Markey say, witnessed a rise in sampling and aggregating physical objects in a *systematic* way, as amassed "collections offered up spaces for individuals to vicariously experience far-flung lands" (213). For Keating and Markey, this *systematization* of the process of collecting material objects and their public display is what is new about the early-modern era, and this is how the early-modern era differs from the preceding medieval period: "While treasuries acted as important spaces for controlling, displaying, and categorizing precious objects in the medieval period, they remained intimate spaces of the religious and princely elite" (213).

Keating and Markey highlight linkages between the rise of the maritime European empires of the early-modern period and artistic production that colluded to render "representations of peoples and monsters on maps," as well as "page after page of detailed woodcuts of peoples from around the

---

[25] Conversely, today's forms of collection, augmented by digital technology, can work to rectify some of the politics of collecting that have characterized museum collections of the imperial past, such as, for example, the collections of the British Museum, with artifacts amassed (or "purloined," depending on your point of view) from all over the British Empire. On www .globalmiddleages.org, Chapurukha Kusimba, an archeologist of East Africa and the Swahili coast, talks about how digital projects on East Africa's artifacts correct the colonial perspective of Africa as a primitive "black continent," by demonstrating the existence of cities and sophisticated urbanism, as well as complex social and trade networks that connect East Africa to global commerce all the way to China.

world dressed in their indigenous clothing" (214). Looking at the picturing of foreign peoples in European art of the time period, Keating and Markey, who are art historians of the early-modern era, believe that "the category of the human was newly invented through cartographic representations" that showed ethnic differences in the sixteenth and seventeenth centuries (214).

Medievalist art historians, of course, have long shown that the category of the human was also invented and reinvented repeatedly in the art of the European medieval world including, spectacularly and memorably, in cartographic representations on *mappaemundi* – maps of the world that depicted Jews, Muslims, Turks, Mongols, Africans, the Plinian monstrous races, and others in surveys of the world's peoples, to establish the boundaries of the human and the civilized.[26]

Indeed, it would seem an impetus of art and culture in each era to invent, and reinvent, the category of the human in a kind of perpetual motion machine of recurrence (like the recurrences of modernity?), but with differences in terms of their *techne*, dispersion, and modalities of expression in each period (however historically conceived) in the many vectors of the world.

9 Globalization, Globalism, World-Systems: The Planet, the Globe, and the World, Part Two

Retaining historical periods, and periodization, in order to recognize epistemic transformations – while carefully identifying differences and continuities *within* periods and *between* periods – as we work to complexify our understanding of the global is one way to ensure that scholars of early global studies do not inadvertently collapse all the different forms that globalism has taken, across centuries and millennia, into a single thing called "globalization."

If we want our scholarly colleagues who have painstakingly conceptualized *globalization* as a description of contemporary, twenty-first century conditions to respect our conceptualizations of premodern eras – including an argument that modernity and globalism are phenomena that recur across deep historical time – we would do well, in return, to reciprocate by honoring the historical and material conditions, the particulars, of *their* era: contemporary time. I explain why in the next section.

Nonetheless, we should recognize that the catchall term, *globalization,* as shorthand for the interconnectedness of the world, has real seductiveness for premodernists. For one thing, "globalization" is a familiar-sounding term that carries significant cultural capital in the academy and in public political discourse today – in part because of the crucial urgencies caused by globalization,

---

[26] See Heng, *Invention of Race*, 33–36.

which pervasively command attention, but partly also because of the brilliance of the academic analysts who study globalization.

Unsurprisingly, scholars have leapt onto the bandwagon of finding globalization everywhere in time. Immanuel Wallerstein, the initiator of world-systems theory – itself a *grand récit* with many followers of its own – looking back from the vantage point of 2004, three decades after the appearance of his influential 1974 volume, *The Modern World System Vol. I,* is even tempted to claim that "the proponents of world-systems analysis" (chief of which is Wallerstein himself) had in fact actually "been talking about globalization since long before the word was invented – not, however, as something new but as something that has been basic to the modern world-system ever since it began in the sixteenth century" (Wallerstein, *World-Systems Analysis* x).[27]

In applying a term and a concept – *globalization* – that coalesced specifically as a description and an analysis of our contemporary moment, Wallerstein is not the only scholar to generalize the term, and to unmoor it from its twenty-first-century coordinates, so that it can be applied more loosely to the past. For Wallerstein, of course, the past that is all-important is the century he sees as the birth of capitalism: the sixteenth century.

For the postcolonial studies scholar Ali Behdad, another modernist, the term *globalization* can be generalized even further back, into premodern time: "[T]he condition we call globalization is not new if viewed historically in the context of colonial relations of power and other earlier world-systems preceding European hegemony since 1492" (63). Behdad thus conjoins *two* catchall terms in presenting the interconnectedness of a premodern world that preceded European hegemony: *globalization* and *world-systems*. My discussion in Sections 10 and 11 unpacks the implications of deploying each of these terms and concepts.

Generalization of the term and concept, *globalization,* to *all* periods of the past as a catchall, bandwagon term for global interconnectedness has, in fact, become increasingly common. In the anthology, *Globalization in World History,* edited by A. G. Hopkins, C. A. Bayly finds "'Archaic' and 'Modern' Globalization in the Eurasian and African Arena, Ca. 1750–1850"; Richard Drayton discusses "Globalizations in the Atlantic World, Ca. 1600–1850"; and Tony Ballantyne discovers "proto-globalization" beginning between 1760 and 1850 (118). The distinguished Sinologist Valerie Hansen has announced in a lively new book that the year 1000 CE is in fact the year when globalization

---

[27] While we need not join Wallerstein in viewing the sixteenth-century world-system as tantamount to globalization, he is an important figure in the development of globalization theory, and world-systems analysis was an important precedent for later economic analyses of globalization, as my discussion in Section 11 will make clear.

began, albeit conceding that, "To be sure, this wasn't globalization in the current sense of the word" (3).

The contributors to another anthology, *Globalization and Global History*, edited by Barry K. Gills and William R. Thompson, transport the term and concept even further back in time. In this anthology, David Wilkinson's essay, "Globalizations: The First Ten, Hundred, Five Thousand and Million Years," applies a very loosely defined "globalization," first to millennial time, and then to primordial time. "The globalization of both world systems and the world economy takes us at least to a 5,000-year timescale," Wilkinson begins, "[s]o there exists a 5,000-year timescale for globalization as a process" (72, 73). Having already claimed 5,000 years of globalization, Wilkinson then suggests that globalization in fact began when homo sapiens sapiens emerged "out of Africa," or began to use fire (73), in what he calls "[t]he longest term globalization process" of all time (74).

When globalization can be said to have begun when homo sapiens sapiens moved out of Africa and began to use fire, what happens to our understanding of what *globalization* actually means?

10 *Globalization*: A Name for Today, but Not for All Time

Scholars of globalization today point to our contemporary moment in time as a new historical formation in which the planet is gridded by technological innovation of such speed and scale as never seen before; in which the sheer density, intensity, and simultaneity of human interconnectivity characterizing our current global moment is recognized as something new; and in which relations of production, consumption, markets, and labor have coalesced into configurations that have not appeared in preceding eras of human civilization.

In making claims that the interconnections of the premodern, prehistoric, or primordial past are tantamount to *globalization*, we would thus be saying that the speed, the scale, the intensity, the technological innovation, the planetary interconnectivity, the digital immediacy, the financial networks, production chains, labor configurations, and the sheer density and contraction of time, distance, and geographic space that characterize our current global moment do not make for meaningful differences. This is not the kind of exercise in retrieving recurrence-across-temporality that premodernists or medievalists should endorse.

When premodernists point to the recurrence-with-difference of phenomena identified as indices of modernity, we carefully point to phenomena that in fact *share a basis* in technology, institutions, methods, or statistical reckoning across time. Thus, early China's precocious modernity is witnessed by print culture in the form of blocks and movable type, paper money, gunpowder, scientific tracking of supernovas, linear algebra, massive use of coal in iron and steel industries, systematized taxation, welfare and census systems, and demographic data, inter alia – all markers of a modernity typically located, in common understanding, only in the West, and only several centuries later.[28]

   To indicate how industrial modernity can recur across seven centuries, Robert Hartwell's use of statistics in meticulous, data-driven scholarly research compares the tonnage of coal burnt in eleventh-century Song China's iron and steel industries with the tonnage of coal burnt in early eighteenth-century Britain's iron and steel industries: a comparison of iron and steel industries similarly driven by *coal*, the fossil fuel utilized in both eras ("A Revolution in the Chinese Iron and Coal Industries"). Hartwell did not claim the recurrence of an industrial modernity by comparing, say, a coal-based industry in China some thousand years ago, and a nuclear-fission-based industry today, to assert that we have always been modern.

Responsible premodernists recognize that technology makes a difference. A planet alive with social media, the Internet, cell phones, global positioning satellites, and supercomputers produces new outcomes materially distinguishable from a time when geographic distance forcibly delayed communication across long time periods of months and years. The compression of time and space experienced today, as David Harvey points out, is something new even for the undisputed centuries of modernity: the result of technological and material transformations of recent duration.

Even as we rejoice in Yo Yo Ma's declaration that the Silk Road (really a braided web of several discrete "silk roads") is the "internet of antiquity," we should retain the piquant resonance of his metaphor without insisting on any literality in the analogy. The "internet" of the Silk Road/s, we understand, is not the same Internet that speeds social media, Wikileaks, Reddit, 8Chan, Anonymous, Facebook, Twitter, Instagram, WhatsApp, TikTok, or SnapChat.

Karimi merchants who plied the Red Sea and Indian Ocean trade in the mercantile capitalism of the medieval period are not the same as a gargantuan corporate Apple or Microsoft outsourcing production and their supply chain to Foxconn at the other end of the world in the People's Republic of China, in today's post-Fordist, just-in-time global economy. Premodern commerce – like

---

[28] Chinese modernity-within-premodernity is not something new in the vast scholarship on premodern China. Even when Chinese studies scholars are not specifically interested in theories of modernity, or do not marvel at the markers of modernity in early China, they rarely overlook the extraordinary nature of the accomplishments seen – at the very least – in the Tang, Song, and Yuan dynasties.

premodern war, pilgrimage, missionary activity, diplomacy – occurred at the speed of camel or ship, horse or wagon, with nothing of the instantaneity of the Internet, fiber-optic telecommunications, or the electronic instantaneity of global financial circuits – the definitive meta-conditions undergirding globalization today.

Unlike Abraham ben Yizu, who had to wait for the next monsoon to bring him a stone frying pan or paper he ordered from Cairo (if the Arab dhow survived the journey to India with its cargo intact), when you order a laptop from Apple in the United States today, a post-Fordist production process instantly kicks into motion, as fiber-optic networks transmit instructions to factory workers in the People's Republic of China to assemble your computer, so that the gleaming, finished product is delivered into your hands a few days later. Just-in-time, post-Fordist manufacturing also means that the *production process itself is now fully global,* supply chains are globalized, and the relations of production are globally dispersed.[29]

The lived conditions of transmigrant labor, moreover, have changed with the advent of new technologies: now, transnational workers can maintain personal, sociocultural relations across time and geographic distance, in their homelands and in the host countries where they labor, connecting local and global in new manifestations of diasporic identity and attachment, and new forms of locatedness. Under globalization, the experience of time and distance is wholly transformed.

Distance is compressed, and no longer exercises the constraints of old on human activity: When a migrant laborer can Skype or Zoom instantly with his family on the other side of the planet, rather than wait for the next monsoon to bring news by ship across the ocean, the world has shrunk in a way that has no precedent in earlier forms of global interconnectedness.[30]

---

[29] Of course, a globalized supply chain and globalized production processes serve a global market: "The power of the global corporation derives from its unique capacity to use finance, technology, and advanced marketing skills to integrate production on a worldwide scale and thus to realize the ancient capitalist dream of One Great Market" (Barnet and Muller 18, cited by Cedric Robinson 319 n.1).

[30] Timothy Brennan calls this "the meaninglessness of distance in a world of instantaneous communication and 'virtuality'" (44). Globalization, of course, does not reach or affect all on the planet equally. Some parts of the world do not participate in globalization, or participate to the same degree as others: The notorious divide between the Global North and the Global South, for instance, testifies to differential impact and outcomes. Like early globalism, globalization today also has "thick" and "thin" forms, or may be altogether invisible, in the varied localities of the world. I have argued for the coexistence of multiple temporalities enfolded within any historical moment, of which early China's precocious modernity-within-premodernity is just one example: In similar fashion, premodern, modern, and postmodern temporalities, cultures, affects, institutions, and practices can coexist today, even within a single society and even under globalization.

Globalization thus points to the complex, often ironic, uneven, and contradict-ory, political-social-cultural outcomes produced by new technologies for which no premodern or early-modern antecedents exist. A post-Fordist, outsourcing, subcontracting, corporatization of the world, with production regimes in speed-sensitive economies of flexible accumulation, has no precedents in premodernity or early modernity; and a compression of space–time that ends distance and shrinks the planet, condensing life and interaction to the point where a single event – in the entertainment industry, in business negotiations, or in MOOC pedagogy – can be experienced simultaneously by people in Bangkok, Rio de Janeiro, and Vladivostok also has no premodern or early-modern precedent.

To insist, therefore, that *globalization* can be an always-already, catchall category across deep geopolitical time is to empty the term of the significance it bears as an economic, social, political, and cultural analysis of the contem-porary present: a moment that manifests not only the distribution of late capitalism and its cultural logic across the world, but also the ironic, flexible, and reversible relations between nation-states that Alan Liu has labeled "post-neo-colonialism."[31]

When scholars suggest that the world has seen an "archaic globalization," a "proto-globalization," and a "modern globalization" in previous eras of history, we see that what *globalization* means, for them, is an *interconnectivity* in earlier centuries and millennia that links places and peoples around the world in lattices of communication and mobility. Used in this general sense to describe the past, the term *globalization* is really a synonym for the interconnectivity of the world and its networks. What is usually intended, then, by *globalization* is really *a global interconnectedness* which might be better referred to as the *globalism* of earlier eras, preceding the *globalization* of today, and preceding, also, Europe's *colonial globality* in the era of the European maritime empires of the sixteenth through nineteenth centuries, before the decolonization movements of the twentieth century.

To attest to the world's interconnectivity as forms of *globality,* or as the *globalism* of different eras, better retains a sense of the *variety* and the *specific character* of the global interconnectivities of all those earlier eras, without yoking all to a single relationship with contemporary globalization and forcing a resemblance. In this fashion, varied forms of globalism are not recruited for a chronology monolithically aimed at the teleological endpoint of the contemporary present.[32]

---

[31] See Liu's brilliant keynote lecture at the Texas Institute for Literary and Textual Studies' Symposium, "The Digital and the Human(ities)."

[32] Although Wallerstein also uses the term "globalization" loosely, to correspond roughly to his "world-system," as we have seen, he also advocates for careful historiographic retrievals of the past that are respectful of context. In his book, *World-Systems Analysis*, he takes pains to respond to criticism of his work that had amassed over decades. He begins by declaring, as we noted earlier, that: "The proponents of world-systems analysis ... have been talking about

And a corollary: Just as we would want the epistemologies of the academy and public culture to afford recognition to the existence of more than a single scientific or industrial revolution in planetary history, we should also afford recognition to our contemporary moment's technological revolutions and socioeconomic and material transformations, with their particular imprint and signature upon our time. To call early forms of globalism *globalization* spectralizes the condition of the planet today, and attenuates *globalization* to a generality that deprives the present of its appropriate mode of analysis.

After all, the abacus and the supercomputer are both technologies for counting, and each is revolutionary in its time. But between the abacus and the supercomputer are such degrees of separation in speed, volume, scale, and complexity as to make for a qualitative difference between the two machines and the cultures and societies the two technologies serve. *Globalization* today attests a difference of this kind in its degrees of separation from the manifold globalisms of the past.

We thus see that *periodization* can be useful for historiographies of the global in this way, as well: to enable the varied modes and patterns of globality issuing in different eras to be differentiated, and disaggregated, so that all need not bear the one name of *globalization* (whether of an antique, archaic, proto-, premodern, prehistoric, primordial, modern, or postmodern kind), in discussing the world's interconnectivity. Critical global studies can lead the way in this, by stitching together historiographies that are attentive to the specificities of the political, economic, and sociocultural outcomes of specific configurations of globalism, including today's.

The value of studying early globalities for those of us who are committed to a critical global studies lies partly in its capacity for analytic revisionism: so that it is possible to attest, for instance, that globalism did not begin only when the West began to exercise maritime power, at the start of what became Europe's centuries of colonial globalism. Honoring the differential character of varied globalisms with attentiveness and recognition, rather than lining up all the globalisms of the past as precursors for the globalization of the present, ensures

---

globalization since long before the word was invented – not, however, as something new but as something that has been basic to the modern world-system ever since it began in the sixteenth century" (x). But while Wallerstein seems to resemble the scholars who loosely name early forms of globalism, *globalization*, he also argues against the over-generalization, and over-application, of a term, and favors the attention to context for which I have been calling: "[U[sing the same name to describe institutions located in different historical systems quite often confuses rather than clarifies analysis. It is better to think of the set of institutions of the modern world-system as contextually specific to it" (*World-Systems Analysis* 25). The same can be said of the institutions of the postmodern world, called *globalization*.

that variety and difference are not collapsed into an invariant chronology issued by a calendar embedded in Western perspectival interests.

11 *World-Systems*: The Why, the When, and the What

But what of *world-systems*, another favorite term and concept invoked by premodernists and modernists alike for naming the interconnectivities of the past? Immanuel Wallerstein devised world-systems analysis in the 1970s as a historiography of the global to counter Eurocentrism; to perform as a counter-narrative to the nation-state as the driver of economic society and international economic relations; and to critique capitalism and the relations of economic inequality entrenched globally by capitalism.

The nation-state as the predominant historical actor and driving agent was the conceptual model at the time when Wallerstein published his first volume on modern world-systems in 1974, *The Modern World-System: Capitalist Agriculture and the Origins of the European World Economy in the Sixteenth Century.* By contrast, "World-systems analysis meant first of all the substitution of a unit of analysis called 'the world-system' for the standard unit of analysis, which was the national state" (Wallerstein, *World-Systems Analysis* 16). The hyphen in "world-systems," Wallerstein emphasizes, is important:

> Note the hyphen in world-system and its two sub-categories, world-economies and world-empires. Putting in the hyphen was intended to under-line that we are talking not about systems, economies, empires *of the* (whole) world, but of systems, economies, empires *that are* a world (but quite possibly, and indeed usually, not encompassing the entire globe). This is a key initial concept to grasp. It says that in "world-systems" we are dealing with a spatial/temporal zone which cuts across many political and cultural units, one that represents an integrated zone of activity and institutions which obey certain systemic rules (Wallerstein, *World-Systems Analysis* 16–17).

Important to Wallerstein was not only the displacement of emphasis on state-centrism, but also the affordance of an analytic tool for the critique of capitalism's production and renewal of unequal economic relations around the world.

At Wallerstein's insistence, capitalism should be identified not only through its traditional markers like ownership of the means of production, creation and expropriation of surpluses through exploitation of labor, or the characteristic disenfranchisement of labor in production processes, but also by the *ceaseless accumulation of capital* which characterizes the modern world economy: a driving motor that supersedes political ideology, religion, governmental control, and other agentic forces that might otherwise exercise power to over-ride the intensive accumulation of capital as the paramount priority.

We are in a capitalist system *only* when the system gives priority to the *endless* accumulation of capital. Using such a definition, only the modern world-system has been a capitalist system ... a capitalist system requires a very special relationship between economic producers and the holders of political power. If the latter are too strong, as in a world-empire, their interests will override those of the economic producers, and the endless accumulation of capital will cease to be a priority. (Wallerstein, *World-Systems Analysis* 24, emphasis added)

For Wallerstein, premodern circuits in which capital is accumulated – the mercantile trading networks of antiquity or the medieval period would be the examples here – thus do not evince the conditions under which the *ceaseless* accumulation of capital is overriding and paramount, as in the modern world, because premodern economic circuits are subject to disruption by political power, religious ideological constraints, and the like. Instead, Wallerstein prefers to name premodern economic societies of exchange and accumulation *world-empires*:

Thus far, I believe, we have had three historical eras on the planet earth. There was the period before 8–10,000 BC about which we still know very little. The world was probably composed of a large number of scattered minisystems. Then, there was the period from 8–10,000 BC to circa 1500 AD. There were in this period multiple instances of coexisting historical systems (of the three main varieties: world-empires, world-economies, minisystems). None of them was "capitalist" in that none of them was based on the structural pressure for the ceaseless accumulation of capital ... . The third period began circa 1500 AD. The aberrant system, our capitalist world-economy, proved aggressive, expansive, and efficacious. Within a few centuries it encompassed the globe. This is where we are today. (Wallerstein, "World System versus World-Systems" 295)

World-systems analysis (Wallerstein prefers world-systems to be seen as an *analysis*, rather than as a *theory*) understands the capitalist world-economy to be made up of zones that comprise "core" centers, "peripheries," and "semi-peripheries" that are linked into unequal relationships that determine the economic dynamics of the world. For Wallerstein, these unequal relations are central to his searing critique of modern capitalism (which he projects as having an end as well as a beginning), but his division of the world into zones of "cores," "peripheries," and "semi-peripheries" has elicited one of the strongest critiques of world-systems analysis, as I discuss below.

Despite Wallerstein's insistence on the *modern* world as the era of global-capitalism-as-ceaseless-accumulation (the second volume of *The Modern World-System* sees him focusing on the years 1600–1750, while his third volume continues the analysis to 1730–1840s), certain scholars have taken the concept of world-systems much further back into the premodern past. Most notable has been Andre Gunder Frank, who together with Barry K. Gills, gathers up a collection of authors for an edited anthology, *The World System: Five Hundred Years or Five Thousand?,* and sums up the arguments for an extended temporal vista in an Introduction by the editors, "The 5,000-Year World System," as well as an afterword, "Rejoinder and Conclusions."

Capital accumulation, Frank and Gills aver, "did not begin or become 'ceaseless' only after 1500 AD, but has been the motor force of the historical process throughout world system history" ("Rejoinder and Conclusions" 297). Arguing that Wallerstein's categories, "and particularly core-periphery, are also applicable to prehistory, the ancient world, and premodern history," Frank and Gills insist that there has in fact only been *one* world system throughout human history: "a continuous world system and its continuous cyclical development" ("The 5,000-Year World System" 7, 10).[33]

According to Frank and Gills, Wallerstein and his followers "underestimate the importance of capital accumulation via trade and the market in the ancient world system," because "there has been widespread underappreciation or underestimation of the role of capital accumulation, markets, the profit motive, 'entrepreneurial elements,' and of long-distance trade for *most* of world history" ("Rejoinder and Conclusions" 298, 301, emphasis in the original). Frank and Gills summon the work of the contributors to their volume to correct this oversight.

Yet, even as Frank and Gills articulate a belief in *cycles* of historical development – an older, less invoked, much criticized historiographic model of world history – we note that the hyphen on which Wallerstein places emphasis has been elided. The editors do not speak of "world-systems," but only of "world systems": that is, not economic systems that *create a world* in themselves (as modern global capitalism's ceaseless accumulation tends to do, according to Wallerstein), but economic systems that only *exist within* the world.

This slippage – barely acknowledged by Frank and Gills in the six chapters of the anthology they jointly or individually contribute – already registers a de facto *generalization* of Wallerstein's world-systems analysis to enable the editors–authors to accommodate the material conditions of the deep historical

---

[33] While Frank and Gills' one-world system importantly reminds modernity-oriented conceptualists like Wallerstein that global interconnections did not begin in the sixteenth century, their offer of a single system persisting across eons reifies their model to the point where its "cycles" of expansion and contraction acquire a mythic, almost faith-based status. Moreover, for those who are not convinced by Wallerstein in the first place, and who view the macrostructure of a "world-system" or "world system" as less an exact description of ontological reality, and more a heuristic projection of an ideal model that is imperfectly articulated with lived human conditions, a belief in "cycles" can seem almost mystical.

past within the compass of Wallerstein's analysis. Wallerstein, of course, notices the slippage:

> Note a detail in word usage that distinguishes Frank and Gills from me. They speak of a "world system." I speak of "world-systems." I use a hyphen; they do not. I use the plural; they do not. They use the singular because, for them, there is and has only been one world system through all of historical time and space .... This brings us to the hyphen. My "world-system" is not a system "in the world" or "of the world." It is a system "that is a world." Hence the hyphen, since "world" is not an attribute of the system. Rather the two words together constitute a single concept. Frank and Gills's system is a world system in an attributive sense, in that it has been tending over time to cover the whole world. (Wallerstein, "World System versus World-Systems" 294–295).

Wallerstein's response to Frank and Gills' volume recognizes the existence throughout the premodern world of profit-based production processes, and profit-based networks of trade and mercantilism. But it also insists on the acknowledgement of a historical break, as economic conditions transform into something recognizable as qualitatively different in the sixteenth century:

> First ... most of the traditional ways of distinguishing capitalism from other previous historical systems used weak distinctions in that they did not hold up under the light of empirical investigations. These traditional *differentiae specificae* included extensive commodity production, profit-seeking enter-prises, wage labor, and a high level of technology. I called these elements "protocapitalism" since, without them as a *part* of the whole, one couldn't have capitalism. But I argue their presence was not enough to call a historical system a capitalist system.
>
> They were not enough because, I argued, each time the agents who used these elements seemed as if they might be able to go further and create a true capitalist system, they were repressed or destroyed in one way or another. And what then distinguishes a self-sustaining long-lived capitalist system, I asked? To which my answer was that the *differentiae specificae* was, and was *only*, that the system was based on a structural priority given and sustained for the *ceaseless* accumulation of capital. Not, I insist, merely for the accumulation of capital, but for the *ceaseless* accumulation of capital. (Wallerstein, "World System versus World-Systems" 292–293, all emphases in the original)

Wallerstein adds that he has no difficulty accepting the existence of what Frank and Gills call "world systems" (without the hyphen) in prehistory, antiquity, or other premodern eras:

> In his article (1990), he [Frank] makes a case for the growth over thousands of years of an interrelated trade network that he calls the "world system."

I believe in fact his account is a fairly acceptable initial and partial outline of what had been happening in the world between 8000 BC (or so) up to 1500 AD. I agree that there were many major nodes of political-economic activity, which I prefer to call "world-empires," and that these world-empires entered into long-distance trade ... with each other. I agree too that these world-empires included in the trading network of the oikumene various zones that were not organized as "world-empires." I even agree that, as a consequence, there may have been some common economic rhythms between them ("World System versus World-Systems" 293–294)

However, Wallerstein asserts: "I do not believe that trade alone makes a system" ("World System versus World-Systems" 294). For Wallerstein, a qualitative difference ensues when the economic attains supremacy above religion and ideology – when the economic *becomes*, in effect, the new religion and ideology in the era of "ceaseless accumulation" that characterizes modern to late capitalism, but not the trade capitalism of earlier periods.[34] A limited concession of a kind follows:

As I said, I do not disagree that, among many of the major "world-empires," there was a growing network of long-distance trade. And perhaps this "crowding-together" accounts in part for the outbreak of the malady that is capitalism [in the sixteenth century]. I say perhaps, because I do not like the teleological implications of this.[35] I prefer my explanation of a fortuitous simultaneity of events.[36] The two modes of explanation are not necessarily incompatible one with the other (Wallerstein, "World System versus World-Systems" 295).

---

[34] In discussing Antonio Gramsci, Stuart Hall calls such ceaseless accumulation "the expanded regime of capital," or "capital accumulation on an expanded scale," which produces what Gramsci calls a "new level of civilization" (52).

[35] In refusing to affirm that a certain tipping point in premodern mercantile capitalism could have produced the conditions that led to the emergence of capitalism proper in the sixteenth century, Wallerstein follows Louis Althusser, who influentially renovated Marxist thought by disengaging the old Marxian teleology that the world had to move through a sequence of economic stages, each producing the next, in a requisite progression toward an economic outcome (e.g., capitalism, revolution, socialism). Like other Althusserians, Wallerstein appears to favor instead "a discontinuous succession of modes of production" (Althusser and Balibar 204) that need not be causally linked, but can be articulated, yet still possess relative autonomy.

[36] The "simultaneity of events" that produced capitalism proper has, of course, received many conceptual treatments. An example: Cedric Robinson, who, like Wallerstein, does not favor a development from the mercantile capitalism of the medieval era to the full-blown capitalism of the modern era, sees ethnoracial and class-inflected differentiations as key to the formation and development of capitalism, which he dubs *racial capitalism* (chapter 1). Postcolonial studies scholars emphasize the mutually constitutive and interlocking relationship between European global imperialism and global capitalism, while Giovanni Arrighi, who traces the genealogy of *finance* capitalism, finds the beginnings of financialization in mid-fifteenth-century Genoa (for the culmination of finance capitalism under globalization today, see Lin and Neely).

Having thus declined to believe in a cyclical model of history in which there has only ever been a single, continuous world system undergoing historical cycles, and having shown he understands the rejection of teleological modes of historiography in the academy, Wallerstein exhibits the kind of conceptual understanding that shows how he was able, two decades earlier, to devise a theory and an analysis of historical materialism – world-systems – that set an important precedent for the emergence of contemporary theories of globalization.

In that same moment, however, Wallerstein also exhibits a wistful romanticism, and concludes his response by articulating an optimism that harks back to the neo-Marxian influences that had led him to conceptualize world-systems analysis in the 1970s:

> Just because it is useful to probe more intelligently into the patterns of the pre-1500 era does not mean we may ignore the unpleasant and dramatic caesura that the creation of a capitalist world-economy imposed on the world. Only if we keep the caesura in mind will we remember that this historical system, like all historical systems, not only had a beginning (or genesis), but that it will have an end. And only then can we concentrate our attention on what kind of successor system we wish to construct (Wallerstein, "World System versus World-Systems" 295–296).[37]

Just as Wallerstein believes the capitalist system had a beginning, so, also, he believes that capitalism will have an end, and be replaced by something else – a belief that some today might consider a kind of utopian longing that is a remnant of 1970s Marxian thought. But Wallerstein's attention to a form of periodization that pivots on a break in world economic systems from the premodern to the modern inserts a useful cautionary reminder to us to *be attentive to the details and material particulars that characterize each historical context*, because "using the same name to describe institutions located in different historical systems quite often confuses rather than clarifies analysis" (Wallerstein, *World-Systems Analysis* 25).

Nonetheless, the fact that world-systems analysis presents a countering narrative to the nation-state as the driving agent of economic relations has proven

---

[37] Frank and Gills have their own brand of romanticism. Like Wallerstein, they reject Eurocentrism, but unlike Wallerstein, they demand a "*universal* human understanding of our one world history" and "affirm that in the future all world-history writing must be *humanocentric* and as objectively as possible assess the overall unity of all human history" ("Rejoinder and Conclusions" 307, emphasis in the original). Among other things, we see that theirs is palpably not a posthumanist project, and does not see the human as one actor in a complex world shaped by numerous agentic forces, including nonhuman forces such as climate, bacteria, the environment, topography, etc. Frank himself reports that one of the editors of the *Festschrift* for Frank, Sing Chew, "insists that my attempts at 'humanocentric' analysis are not enough. What we need, he says, is 'ecocentric' theory *and praxis*" (Frank xxvi, emphasis in the original).

attractive to medievalists in particular – scholars for whom the time frame of their research and study extends over eras *prior* to the existence of nation-states altogether.[38]

Medievalists who are excited about the global turn in medieval studies thus sometimes invoke Janet L. Abu-Lughod's *Before European Hegemony: The World System A.D. 1250–1350*, a volume that embraces Wallerstein's aim of countering Eurocentrism by highlighting traceries of trade, manufacturing, and mercantile networks around the world from roughly the middle of the thirteenth through the middle of the fourteenth century.

Before European Hegemony is much cited by medievalists of all stripes;[39] the book's famous illustration depicting eight rubber-band-like, stretched circles encompassing regional zones of trading, commerce, and connection that capture core–periphery relationships inside their elongated circles, is often reproduced by those who, following Abu-Lughod, also invoke world-systems as their way to understand premodern globalism. Often, scholars who invoke *Before European Hegemony* believe that the book practices world-systems analysis, and extends world-systems analysis to the medieval past, and that, therefore, world-systems analysis can be unproblematically embraced.

Indeed, Abu-Lughod's essay in Frank and Gills' anthology explicitly says that *Before European Hegemony* was written as a corrective, and an extension, of Wallerstein's world-systems analysis:

> I've recently published a book on the world system in the thirteenth century, entitled *Before European Hegemony*. It was intended in part as a corrective to Immanuel Wallerstein's work on the sixteenth century *et seq.* world-system. My criticism was that Wallerstein, while creatively extending the work of other historians and correcting for some of their biases, had still accepted the main line of western historical scholarship: namely, that the "story" becomes interesting *only* with the "Rise of the West" after 1450.
>
> This, I contend, is much too late. Because his account begins essentially with the sixteenth century, Wallerstein tends to overemphasize the *discontinuity* between the new Eurocentered capitalist world economy that began to come into being then and the system of world-empires and world-economies that had preceded it. And what is less defensible, he refuses to "dignify" any pre-sixteenth-century patterns of global trade by applying the term "world-system" to them. Indeed, he defends reserving *that* term only for the *modern*

---

[38] While medievalists have argued for the emergence of medieval-style *nations* pre-1500 CE – in part by deploying Ben Anderson's definition of the nation as an imagined political community – they have been careful not to claim that medieval imagined communities in fact constituted *nation-states* per se. See, for example, Forde, Johnson, and Murray; Bjørn, Grant, and Stringer; Turville-Petre; Lavezzo; and Heng, *Empire of Magic*, chapters 2 and 4.

[39] Including this author, in chapters 2 and 5 of Heng, *Empire of Magic*, and extensively in chapter 3 of Heng, *Invention of Race*.

world-system, with its capitalist structure ("Discontinuities and Persistence" 278, all emphases in the original)

As someone who has also repeatedly urged modernist colleagues to acknowledge the vital importance of the medieval period, I am wholly in sympathy with Abu-Lughod's indignation at Wallerstein's disregard of premodernity, and profoundly admire the deep historical scholarship of *Before European Hegemony*, a book that remains invaluable for many reasons, including its contribution to anti-Eurocentrism.

Abu-Lughod inveighs mightily against the bias she sees threading through Wallerstein's work: scholarship that shunts aside premodernity as a time of little consequence, and exhibits a modernist bias I have also critiqued at length (see Heng, *Invention of Race* chapter 1). Calling attention to the importance of premodern eras, this Element and the Cambridge Elements series in the Global Middle Ages in general thus share the same aims as Abu-Lughod, even when, occasionally, our strategies or understanding may follow asymptotic trajectories.

Our strategies and understanding do, in fact, diverge in a few important ways. For example, while Abu-Lughod's essay sees continuity and persistence through time, this Element emphasizes recurrences-with-difference across macrohistorical time.[40] In addition, like the scholars who invoke *globalization* in premodernity as a generalized synonym for a *global interconnectedness*, Abu-Lughod's understanding of what world-systems means also effects a generalization, and, moreover, rewrites world-systems analysis into something that is quite different from Wallerstein's conceptualization.

For instance, altogether ignoring the important distinction made by Wallerstein to distinguish his *world-systems* (a capitalist system that forms a world in itself) from Frank and Gills' *world systems* (an economic or trade system that exists within the larger world), Abu-Lughod uses *both* "world

---

[40] Fortunately, Abu-Lughod's preference for historical continuity (in opposition to the historical break that Wallerstein sees as characterizing the onset of the capitalist world-system) does not require her to accept Frank and Gills' notion of 5,000 years of continuity in a single world system evolving through cycles across the millennia. Instead, she cautiously stakes an intermediate position between Wallerstein's *world-system* and Frank and Gills' *world system*, though here as elsewhere, she does not see the distinction between the two kinds of systems invoked – the system with, and the system without, that key hyphen after "world":

"1. Has there been *only one* world-system, the one that began in the *sixteenth century*?

2. Have there been *several successive world-systems*, each with a changing structure and its own set of hegemons?

3. Or has there been only *a single world-system* that has continued to evolve *over the past 5,000 years*?

Wallerstein espouses the first position, I have taken the second, and Frank and Gills contend the third" (Abu-Lughod, "Discontinuities and Persistence" 279, all emphases in the original).

system" and "world-system" interchangeably, as if they have the same referent, and mean the same thing, when they do not. *Before European Hegemony* has Frank and Gills' "world system" in the book's very title, and her essay for their anthology also has "world system" in its subtitle.

But throughout her essay itself, Abu-Lughod repeatedly refers to "world-systems," as if a distinction between the two concepts is not meaningful. Here is an example:

> my position is that a very advanced world-system already existed by the second half of the thirteenth century, one that included almost all regions (only the "New World" was missing) that would be reintegrated in the sixteenth century. Indeed, nascent capitalism was present in various parts of that system, without actually succeeding in dominating all parts ("Discontinuities and Persistence" 278).

In the same way, Abu-Lughod also seems not to see a difference between Wallerstein's understanding of capitalism as identified by *a ceaseless accumulation that overrides all other powers, ideologies, and priorities in its time*, and the mercantile version that characterizes the premodern era – which she calls "nascent capitalism" ("Discontinuities and Persistence" 278), and Wallerstein calls "protocapitalism" ("World System versus World-Systems" 293).

A "nascent" or "proto-" capitalism is not the same thing as the full-blown capitalism of Wallerstein's world-systems analysis. If premodernity witnessed only a "nascent" capitalism, then its world-economy really does lie on the other side of the divide from Wallerstein's capitalist world-economy of the sixteenth century and later, as he has repeatedly said. That is to say, Abu-Lughod's formulation does not so much *correct* Wallerstein's model, as it *confirms* the model as correct.

Moreover, despite her stated intention to counter Wallerstein's positing of a break ("discontinuity") in the world-economy around the time of the sixteenth century, Abu-Lughod concedes that the continuity she sees between the "nascent capitalism" of the medieval period and the full-blown capitalism that Wallerstein sees in the modern period is best witnessed in *local–regional* ambits, rather than in an international (or "world") context:

> On a regional (or what I have called a subsystem) level, one can argue not only for *continuity* but even development and expansion of economic and cultural linkages, without having to assume that the international system itself exhibited such continuities. To put it another way, one might find that local patterns persist and even prosper, while, at the same time, acknowledging that the role of the local region in a wider system has undergone a real transformation. ("Discontinuities and Persistence" 279, emphasis in the original)

Here, Abu-Llughod plainly says there is no need "to assume that the international system itself" exhibits the "continuities" she sees occurring at a *regional* or "subsystem" level; indeed, it is only "local patterns [that] persist and even prosper." Wallerstein's description of a break that produces a new world-system is largely confirmed (the "wider system has undergone a real transformation"), rather than corrected or modified, since Abu-Llughod's argument applies, it seems, to "local patterns" and regional subsystems.

Given these admissions, we should see *Before European Hegemony* not so much as a corrective and an extension of world-systems analysis, but as a volume that surveys *regional subsystems* and their economic interrelationships around the premodern world. This is perhaps a better way to view the book – as a description of how regional subsystems persist and develop through time. Therefore, despite the fact that *Before European Hegemony* invokes world-systems analysis, the author's own description of her book suggests that it really offers *subsystems analysis*: a framework to see how local–regional ecosystems of manufacturing-trading-societal relations intersected and existed in a world characterized by mercantile ("nascent" or "proto-"?) capitalism.

A survey of this kind, which studies the discrete, parallel, and/or intersecting regional subsystems that interacted and thrived for a time in the premodern world, makes an invaluable contribution indeed; but it is not world-systems theory, and should not be taken as an example of world-systems analysis as such. A final concession from Abu-Lughod clinches the point.

Both in her book and her essay, Abu-Lughod sketches a historiographic trajectory in which the importance of the East wanes toward the end of the medieval period, as the West ascends to dominance – a process that Euromedievalists have sometimes dubbed *translatio imperii,* the movement, or westering, of empire. Abu-Lughod presents several persuasive reasons for "the fall of the East" and the "rise of the West" – military, epidemiological, technological factors, and more – that caused "the containing system [to] drastically [alter] after the middle of the fourteenth century and especially after the fifteenth century. It would be totally transformed by the sixteenth" ("Discontinuities and Persistence" 288, 284).

This paradigm of a falling East (starting in the mid-fourteenth century) and a rising West (culminating in a world "totally transformed" by the sixteenth century) again fits neatly into Wallerstein's world-systems paradigm: In the sixteenth century, according to Wallerstein, the world is, indeed, totally transformed by the rise of capitalism, a relentless system of ceaseless accumulation as the priority that overrides state, religion, and all ideologies of power, to position first Europe, then the West, and finally the Global North in relations of economic dominance in the world. Rather than counter Wallerstein's argument that a historical transformation occurred between the premodern and modern periods, Abu-Lughod's fall-of-the-East-and-rise-of-the-West narrative *confirms* that a break did occur, and the world's systems are "totally transformed" by the sixteenth century.[41]

Before European Hegemony is thus most usefully seen as an un-Eurocentric description of regional subsystems that intersect or overlap in the medieval world, rather than as an exemplar of world-systems analysis corrected for the premodern, and applied to the centuries we think of as medieval. But here, too, scholars who would apply the book's thinking should be cognizant of certain other problematic features.

First of all, although Abu-Lughod speaks of a "very advanced world-system [which] existed by the second half of the thirteenth century ... that included almost all regions" where "only the 'New World' was missing," her eight elongated ovals illustrating zones containing core–periphery relations are missing more than just the "New World." The important zones of Oceania and Austronesia are also missing, as is much of the continent of Africa – all of which are also active zones of exchange.[42] Lately, these omissions have increasingly been noted:

> Her schema consisted of eight interlocking spheres, stretching from western Europe and centered on the Champagne fairs, through the Mediterranean and multiple Islamic systems, to the Far East. West Africa, however, sits forlorn and uncircumscribed on her diagram, while the trans-Saharan trade that furnished the Mediterranean basin, and all of its interconnecting systems, with the economic lubricant of gold is conspicuously absent (Guérin 98).

---

[41] By contrast, Frank's later, highly influential book, *ReOrient: Global Economy in the Asian Age*, which focuses on the early-modern world, suggests that Asia's "decline" or "fall" did not begin until the nineteenth century: "Asia, and especially China and India, but also Southeast Asia and West Asia, were more active, and the first three also more important to [the] world economy than Europe was until about 1800" (*ReOrient* xxiv). *ReOrient*, an important study for its sustained concentration on the many Asias, continues to dispute Wallerstein's positioning of a break in the sixteenth century world economy, and argues that while a break might have occurred for Europe, it did not occur for Asian world systems until centuries later. Frank thereby intimates that, ironically, Wallerstein's world-systems analysis is Eurocentric in its own way, even as world-systems analysis aims to counter Eurocentrism.

[42] The Cambridge Elements in the Global Middle Ages series will correct some of these lacunae, without reissuing the "core–periphery" economic model that replicates world-systems analysis. Pauketat and Alt, among others, have sketched trade, religious, and architectural interactions between early Mexican–Central American polities and southwestern and midwestern polities on the North American continent. James Flexner's Element, *Oceania: 800–1800 CE: A Millennium of Interactions in a Sea of Islands*, stresses that for the inhabitants of Oceania, dispersed across half the world, the ocean represented not a boundary or obstacle, but a fluid medium for long-distance interactions and a bountiful resource; the worlds of Polynesia evince ongoing patterns of inter-island voyaging, trade, intermarriage, conflict, and settlement, while those of Melanesia see the development of specialized trade and exchange networks as a recurring theme.

Beyond the remarkable absence of West Africa – a key zone of production, trade, and exchange that has been extensively documented by archeologists and, more recently and to spectacular visual effect, by the "Caravans of Gold" exhibition at Northwestern University's Block Museum, curated by Kathleen Bickford Berzock – most of the African continent outside the Mediterranean North and the Horn are blank, their exchanges with the world untold. The Swahili coast, a rich area of trade and exchange, as archeologists have demonstrated, is also a blank on the map, like the rest of Saharan Africa. In lieu of a Dark Continent, we have a largely Blank Africa.[43]

Moreover, Abu-Lughod's endorsement of core-and-periphery as the favored model for reckoning the premodern world's economic relations in the form of eight regional circuits is also problematic in other ways. This is because a persistent critique leveled at world-systems analysis is that the spatial division of the world into core–periphery-and-semi-periphery is simplistic and crude, and fails to account for finer-grained economic relations, even as it passes over more complex and nuanced accounts of the international economy of the modern world.

Carving up the *pre*modern world through an optic of center–periphery relations replicates all the shortcomings of Wallerstein's model of the modern world, but without securing the advantage of his model as a materialist critique of modern global capitalism. Even if we were to add a *ninth* elongated circle to Abu-Lughod's famous illustration of regional circuits that would rope, say, at least West Africa into relationship with the metropolis of Cairo and Maghrebi North Africa, the very idea that there are "core" centers and "peripheral" outer zones is an idea that many would likely find objectionable, even offensive.

What criteria decide that an area is central, constituting a "core," while other areas are outlying, constituting mere "peripheries"? Some kinds of manufacturing, production processes, and products, over other kinds, as Wallerstein suggests? Or, extrapolating beyond Wallerstein, criteria such as the presence of cities of a certain size or complexity? How would we define complexity in urban centers? Through wealth? And what can be reckoned an area's wealth – land? gold? people? a favorable balance-of-payments calculus?

An optic of center–periphery relations can end up consigning certain zones of the world – like Saharan Africa, for instance – to a status that overrecognizes the extraction of their natural resources and raw materials (identifying such zones

---

[43] For a sense of the wide-ranging work accomplished by archeologists of premodern Saharan Africa, see, especially, Aluka (www.aluka.org/heritage), the Zamani project (www.zamaniproject.org), and the East Africa project (www.globalmiddleages.org/project/early-global-connections-east-africa-between-asia-and-mediterranean-europe).

as producers merely of "peripheral products") and underrecognizes their complex economic agency, the sophistication of their manufactures, and their role in regional and international economies. This can easily create an impression of the underperformance of certain zones relative to the so-called all-important civilizational metropoles ("great global cities") located elsewhere (identified as the producers of "core-like products"), instead of unearthing the fine-grained complexity of interregional and international economic interactions.

The deck can thus be stacked against the zones some scholars study, not only by the metropoles of the premodern past, but also by the core–periphery model that is set in place as the appropriate model of analysis for studying the premodern world's economic relations. Of course, the ever-careful Wallerstein reminds us that "core" and "periphery" are intended only to designate production processes, not particular zones, regions, countries, or polities: "[O]ne could use a shorthand language by talking of core and peripheral zones (or even core and peripheral states), as long as one remembered that it was *the production processes and not the states* that were core-like and peripheral" (*World-Systems Analysis* 17, emphasis added).

While Wallerstein is astute in specifying that we should not infer a status of superiority or subordination (or relative importance?) among polities, states, and regions from their designation by world-systems models as either "core" or "periphery" or "semi-periphery" – which are designations, apparently, that only indicate a zone's *production processes* – in actual discussion a distinction of this kind is easily elided.

Should students be guided to study "core" zones that have been identified as central to regional economies and the world-economy, or can we trust that they will still be recruited to academic positions if they study what are deemed to be the "peripheral" areas of the world? Perhaps more is at stake than just the naming of production processes. We have here, again, yet another reminder that *names, and what they indicate,* continue to matter. Why would we need to see centers and peripheries at all in premodern economic relations, when the very aim – the promise – of a critical early global studies is precisely to deliver an uncentered world? For those who inhabit the world, *everywhere* is the center of the world; everywhere is a "core."

There are other reasons why premodernists should be wary of embracing world-systems analysis as a heuristic model for the premodern world. World-systems analysis has also been criticized for its reduction of explanations to economic factors; for its failure to articulate economic relations with wider, sociocultural contexts; and for its lack of a sophisticated engagement with cultural dimensions of historical explanation. Its Marxian residue also means that world-systems analysis is also, of course, at base another totalizing *grand récit*. About this, Wallerstein is unapologetic: "Of course, world-systems analysis is . . . a grand narrative . . . .but . . . some grand narratives reflect reality more closely than others" (World-Systems Analysis 21).

Whether world-systems analysis can "reflect reality" in modern eras will no doubt continue to be dialectically discussed, but it may be that grand narratives serve the study of early globalism less finely than a plethora of other historiographic tools that include the accumulation of microhistories, the collection of histories-from-below, and the investigation of unread or insufficiently read archives, to compile a variegated view of the interconnected past – in contradistinction to the totalizing and schematic accounts that grand narratives deliver.

In particular, for those averse to privileging the economic as an all-determinative macrostructure, the explanatory functionalism offered by a grand narrative of economic relations may capture less than satisfactorily the untidy fluidity and unpredictability of lived realities. Life on the ground seems always, and notoriously, in excess of schematic accounts.

In this, Amitav Ghosh's drive to extract the circumstances of a single, individual, enslaved person's life, out of the anonymity of an 800-year-old global past, and to make that life intelligible to twentieth-century subaltern studies, might be seen as one example of an alternative way to retrieve the conditions of early globalism without recourse to grand schemas.

Teaching himself twelfth-century Hebraicized Arabic and its paleography, Ghosh combs out of the recesses of the twelfth-century Indian Ocean world of trading relations: the quotidian data of individual lives, everyday domestic conditions, a minutiae of household possessions, the intricate play of obligations in far-flung business partnerships, glimmers of what marriage and family life might look like, and the all-important, crucially determinative role of monsoons and weather in human interactions.

This kind of perspective of the global, teased out of so many fine details and a historiography that works by building up evidence from traces, fragments, and clues in surviving documents and artifacts to piece together global interconnections, stands as a resonant alternative to the schematics of macrostructural *grand-récit* historiography in retrieving a variegated world of interrelationships whose fine-grained complexity, intricacy, and density of detail is not overlooked.

The way seems clear: beyond economic macrostructures pitched at high altitude, the recovery of a global past in deep time needs to be thickened by close-up studies of the connective warp and weave of culture, society, religion, climate, animals, plants, bacteria, ecoscapes, architecture, art, music, class, gender, sexuality, race, stories – that whole human life cycle and environmental habitus of earlier worlds.

12 Worlds of Differences: The Cambridge Elements in the Global Middle Ages: Collaboration, Experimentation, and an Open-Ended Process

To recover the variegated worlds of the deep global past, this Cambridge Elements series in the Global Middle Ages aims to deliver to readers ideas, guidelines, arguments, speculations, experiments, interventions, and perspectives on early globalism in an open-ended process wherein collaboration is often embraced as a key operational modality of how we research, teach, study, and learn about the deep global past.

Our work on the Global Middle Ages Projects for almost two decades has pivoted on successful collaboration in teaching, digital projects, research, conferences and workshops, and more. A number of our Elements authors have aleady collaborated with us in other contexts: in projects of experimental teaching, digital humanities projects, workshops, grants, and symposia. Many of the titles in this Cambridge Elements series are coauthored by teams of scholars, working in pairs or groups of three and four, to present the worlds they know best. Invariably, of course, some subjects are so large and complex that even a team of three or four authors, working together on an Element, can feel its limitations. These subjects may need a number of Elements, and perhaps clusters of Elements.

But unlike the gigantic textbooks on global history that are the common means for teaching the deep past in classrooms today – costly tomes that offer broad surveys across vast geographic spans and timelines, and that have to be continually repurchased every few years as new editions supersede older ones – each Element in our series offers both a survey and an in-depth analysis in a compact study of around 30,000 words. Elements are inexpensive, and highly customizable to readers' individual needs for self-education, teaching, or research, and are updatable annually, as their authors wish.

Importantly, Elements are also born-digital (with print as an option), and can embed audio, video, images, podcasts, digital projects, lectures, and the like. One pair of Elements, on early and later Tang China and the World, embeds an ArcGIS mapping project with story maps. In many ways, we believe Elements point to the future of publishing, where the aim is to furnish a *customizable* set of materials that can be personalized for a variety of readerly needs. The born-digital character of these Elements also ensures their continual updatability, and provides a robust textual environment that is hospitable to incorporating enriched digital media and technology as new technologies and media emerge and become available.

Like the platform of the Global Middle Ages Project at www.globalm-iddleages.org (a platform we affectionately refer to as *MappaMundi*), these

Cambridge Elements do not aggregate a grand narrative of early globalism, but together sketch a variegated mosaic of the global past in deep history, without privileging zones, regions, oceans, or societies; types of economic or other forms of organization; or types of *habitus* or environments. Authorial styles and emphases, disciplinary assumptions and methods, forms of analysis, and ways of seeing will differ from Element to Element: The recovery of a world of differences cannot occur through a homogeneity of method, nor an empire of style.

As we plan and deliver Elements that open windows onto the worlds of early globalism, we invite ideas, suggestions, and feedback, as well as prospective collaboration with a large and growing international community of scholars. Together, we, authors and readers alike – and most of us will always be both authors and readers – have nothing to lose but our provincialism.

References

Abu-Lughod, Janet L. *Before European Hegemony: The World System AD 1250–1350*. Oxford University Press, 1989.

"Discontinuities and Persistence: One World System or a Succession of Systems?" *The World System: Five Hundred Years or Five Thousand?*, edited by Andre Gunder Frank and Barry K. Gills, Routledge, 1993, pp. 278–291.

Achi, Andrea Myers, and Seeta Chaganti. "'Semper Novi Quid ex Africa': Redrawing the Borders of Medieval African Art and Considering Its Implications for Medieval Studies." *Disturbing Times: Medieval Pasts, Reimagined Futures*, edited by Catherine E. Karkov, Anna Klosowska, and Vincent W. J. van Gerven Ooi, Punctum Books, 2020, pp. 73–106.

Althusser, Louis, and Étienne Balibar. *Reading Capital*. New Left Books, 1970.

Anderson, Benedict. *Imagined Communities: Reflections on the Origins and Spread of Nationalism*. Verso, 1991.

Armitage, Hanae. "Polynesians, Native Americans Made Contact before European Arrival, Genetic Study Finds." *Stanford Medicine News Center*, July 8, 2020, http://med.stanford.edu/news/all-news/2020/07/polynesians-and-native-americans-made-early-contact.html. Accessed July 9, 2020.

Arrighi, Giovanni. *The Long Twentieth Century: Money, Power, and the Origins of our Times*. Verso, 1994, 2nd ed., 2010.

Ballantyne, Tony. "Empire, Knowledge, and Culture: From Proto-Globalization to Modern Globalization." *Globalization in World History*, edited by A. G. Hopkins, Norton, 2002, pp. 116–140.

Barker, Hannah. *That Most Precious Merchandise: The Mediterranean Trade in Black Sea Slaves, 1260–1500*. University of Pennsylvania Press, 2019.

Barnet, Richard, and Ronald Muller. *Global Reach*. Simon and Schuster, 1974.

Bayly, C. A. "'Archaic' and 'Modern' Globalization in the Eurasian and African Arena, ca. 1750–1850." *Globalization in World History*, edited by A. G. Hopkins, Norton, 2002, pp. 45–72.

Behdad, Ali. "On Globalization, Again!" *Postcolonial Studies and Beyond*, edited by Ania Loomba, Suvir Kaul, Matti Bunzi, Antoinette Burton, and Jed Esty, Duke University Press, 2005, pp. 62–79.

Berzock, Kathleen Bickford. *Caravans of Gold, Fragments in Time: Art, Culture, and Exchange across Medieval Saharan Africa*. Block Museum of Art, Northwestern University, in association with Princeton University Press, 2019.

Biagioli, Mario. "The Scientific Revolution Is Undead." *Configurations*, vol. 6, no. 2, 1998, pp. 141–148.

Bjørn, Claus, Alexander Grant, and Keith J. Stringer, editors. *Nations, Nationalism, and Patriotism in the European Past*. Copenhagen, Academic Press, 1994.

Brennan, Timothy. "Postcolonial Studies and Globalization Theory." *The Postcolonial and the Global*, edited by Revathi Krishnaswamy and John C. Hawley, University of Minnesota Press, 2008, pp. 37–53.

Chaganti, Seeta. "Solidarity and the Medieval Invention of Race." *Cambridge Journal of Postcolonial Literary Inquiry*, forthcoming.

Cheng, Bonnie. "A Camel's Pace: A Cautionary Global." *Re-Assessing the Global Turn in Medieval Art History*, edited by Christina Normore. Arc Humanities Press, 2018, pp. 11–34.

Clifford, James. *The Predicament of Culture: Twentieth-Century Ethnography, Literature, and Art*. Harvard University Press, 1988.

Constable, Olivia Remie. "Muslim Spain and Mediterranean Slavery: The Medieval Slave Trade as an Aspect of Muslim-Christian Relations." *Christendom and Its Discontents: Exclusion, Persecution, and Rebellion, 1000–1500*, edited by Scott L. Waugh and Peter D. Diehl, Cambridge University Press, 1996, pp. 264–284.

Davidson, Cathy N. "Strangers on a Train: A Chance Encounter Provides a Lesson in Complicity and the Never-Ending Crisis in the Humanities." *Academe*, September–October 2001, www.aaup.org/article/strangers-train#.Xu7_1i2ZPOQ. Accessed July 18, 2020.

Devisse, Jean. *The Image of the Black in Western Art: From the Early Christian Era to the "Age of Discovery," Vol. 2, Part 1: From the Demonic Threat to the Incarnation of Sainthood*. Translated by William G. Ryan, William Morrow, 1979.

Dhar, Amrita. "*The Invention of Race* and the Postcolonial Renaissance." *Cambridge Journal of Postcolonial Literary Inquiry*, forthcoming.

Dimock, Wai Chee. *Through Other Continents: American Literature across Deep Time*. Princeton University Press, 2006.

Drayton, Richard. "The Collaboration of Labor: Slaves, Empires, and Globalizations in the Atlantic World, ca. 1600–1850." *Globalization in World History*, edited by A. G. Hopkins, Norton, 2002, pp. 99–115.

Epstein, Steven A. *Speaking of Slavery: Color, Ethnicity, and Human Bondage in Italy*. Cornell University Press, 2001.

Flatt, Emma J. "The Worlds of South Asia." *Teaching the Global Middle Ages*, edited by Geraldine Heng, The Modern Language Association of America, forthcoming.

Forde, Simon, Lesley Johnson, and Alan V. Murray, editors. *Concepts of National Identity in the Middle Ages*. University of Leeds Press, 1995.

Frank, Andre Gunder. *ReOrient: Global Economy in the Asian Age*. University of California Press, 1998.

Frank, Andre Gunder and Barry K. Gills. "The 5,000-Year World System: An Interdisciplinary Introduction." *The World System: Five Hundred Years or Five Thousand?*, edited by Andre Gunder Frank and Barry K. Gills. Routledge, 1993, pp. 3–58.

"Rejoinder and Conclusions." *The World System: Five Hundred Years or Five Thousand*, edited by Andre Gunder Frank and Barry K. Gills. Routledge, 1993, pp. 297–307.

editors. *The World System: Five Hundred Years or Five Thousand?* Routledge, 1993.

Friedman, Susan Stanford. *Planetary Modernisms: Provocations on Modernity across Time*. Columbia University Press, 2018.

Galbraith, Kate. "British 'Medievalists' Draw Their Swords." *Chronicle of Higher Education*, June 6, 2003, A42.

Ghosh, Amitav. *In an Antique Land: History in the Guise of a Traveler's Tale*. Granta, 1992.

"The Slave of MS. H.6." *Subaltern Studies VII: Writings on South Asian History and Society*, edited by Partha Chatterjee and Gyanendra Pandey, Oxford University Press, 1993, pp. 159–220.

Gills, Barry K. and William R. Thompson, editors. *Globalization and Global History*. Routledge, 2006.

Goitein, S. D. and Mordechai Akiva Friedman, editors and translators. *India Traders of the Middle Ages: Documents from the Cairo Geniza ("India Book")*. Brill, 2008.

Goldstone, Jack A. "Efflorescences and Economic Growth in World History: Rethinking the 'Rise of the West' and the Industrial Revolution." *Journal of World History*, vol. 13, no. 2, 2002, pp. 323–389.

Grewal, Inderpal. "Amitav Ghosh: Cosmopolitanisms, Literature, Transnationalisms." *The Postcolonial and the Global*, edited by Revathi Krishnaswamy and John C. Hawley, University of Minnesota Press, 2008, pp. 178–190.

Guérin, Sarah M. "Exchange of Sacrifices: West Africa in the Medieval World of Goods." *Re-Assessing the Global Turn in Medieval Art History*, edited by Christina Normore, Arc Humanities Press, 2018., pp. 97–115.

Hall, Stuart. "Race, Articulation, and Societies Structured in Dominance." *Race Critical Theories*, edited by Philomena Essed and David Theo Goldberg,

Blackwell, 2002, pp. 38–68. Reprinted from UNESCO, *Sociological Theories: Race and Colonialism*. UNESCO, 1980, pp. 305–345.

Hansen, Valerie. *The Year 1000: When Explorers Connected the World – and Globalization Began*. Scribner, 2020.

Hart, Roger. *The Chinese Roots of Linear Algebra*. Johns Hopkins University Press, 2010.

"The Great Explanandum." *The American Historical Review*, vol. 105, no. 2, 2000, pp. 486–493.

Hartwell, Robert. "A Cycle of Economic Change in Imperial China: Coal and Iron in Northeast China, 750–1350." *Journal of the Social and Economic History of the Orient*, vol. 10, 1967, pp. 102–159.

"A Revolution in the Chinese Iron and Coal Industries during the Northern Sung, 960–1126 A.D." *Journal of Asian Studies*, vol. 21, no. 2, 1962, pp. 153–162.

Harvey, David. *The Condition of Postmodernity*. Blackwell, 1990.

Heng, Geraldine. "An Experiment in Collaborative Humanities: Imagining the World 500–1500." *ADFL Bulletin*, vol. 38, no. 3, 2007, pp. 20–28.

"An Ordinary Ship and Its Stories of Early Globalism: Modernity, Mass Production, and Art in the Global Middle Ages." *The Journal of Medieval Worlds*, vol. 1 no. 1, 2019, pp. 11–54.

"Global Interconnections: Imagining the World 500–1500." Medieval Academy Newsletter, September 2004.

"Reinventing Race, Colonization, and Globalisms across Deep Time: Lessons from the *Longue Durée*." *PMLA*, vol. 130, no. 2, 2015, 358–366.

"The Global Middle Ages." *Experimental Literary Education*, special issue of *English Language Notes*, vol. 47, no. 1, 2009, pp. 205–216.

The Invention of Race in the European Middle Ages. Cambridge University Press, 2018.

Holsinger, Bruce W. *Neomedievalism, Neoconservatism, and the War on Terror*. Prickly Paradigm, 2007.

Hopkins, A. G., editor. *Globalization in World History*. Norton, 2002.

Ioannidis, Alexander G., et al. "Native American Gene Flow into Polynesia Predating Easter Island Settlement." *Nature*, July 8, 2020, https://doi.org/10.1038/s41586-020-2487-2. Accessed July 9, 2020.

Johnston, Neil. "Leicester University Considers Lessons in Diversity as Medieval Studies Axed." *The Sunday Times*, February 5, 2021, www.thetimes.co.uk/article/leicester-university-considers-lessons-in-diversity-as-medieval-studies-axed-nsrs2hvf0. Accessed February 6, 2021.

Kaplan, Paul H. D. *The Rise of the Black Magus in Western Art*. UMI Research Press, 1985.

Keating, Jessica and Lia Markey. "Response: Medievalists and Early Modernists – A World Divided?" *Re-Assessing the Global Turn in Medieval Art History*, edited by Christina Normore, Arc Humanities Press, 2018, pp. 203–217.

Keene, Bryan C., editor. *Toward a Global Middle Ages: Encountering the World through Illuminated Manuscripts*. The J. Paul Getty Museum, 2019.

Kim, Dorothy. "White Supremacists Have Weaponized an Imaginary Viking Past. It's Time to Reclaim the Real History." *Time*, April 14, 2019, https://time.com/5569399/viking-history-white-nationalists/. Accessed July 9, 2020.

Krishnan, Sanjay. *Reading the Global: Troubling Perspectives in Britain's Empire in Asia*. Columbia University Press, 2007.

Lampert, Lisa. "Race, Periodicity, and the (Neo-) Middle Ages." *Modern Language Quarterly*, vol.65, 2004, pp. 392–421.

Lavezzo, Kathy, editor. *Imagining a Medieval English Nation*. University of Minnesota Press, 2004.

Lin, Ken-Hou and Megan Tobias Neely. *Divested: Inequality in the Age of Finance*. Oxford University Press, 2020.

Liu, Alan. "The University in the Digital Age: The Big Questions." The Digital and the Human(ities), Symposium II, Teaching and Learning, Keynote Lecture, March 10, 2011, Texas Institute for Literary and Textual Studies 2010–11, www.youtube.com/watch?v=RALNyQL0kTY. Accessed July 19, 2020.

Lomuto, Sierra. "Public Medievalism and the Rigor of Anti-Racist Critique." *In the Middle*, April 4, 2019, https://www.inthemedievalmiddle.com/2019/04/public-medievalism-and-rigor-of-anti.html. Accessed July 13, 2020.

—— "White Nationalism and the Ethics of Medieval Studies." *In the Middle*, December 5, 2016, https://www.inthemedievalmiddle.com/2016/12/white-nationalism-and-ethics-of.html. Accessed July 9, 2020.

Margaryan, Ashot, et al. "Population Genomics of the Viking World." *Nature*, vol. 585, 2020, pp. 390–396.

Mullaney, Thomas S., et al., editors. *Critical Han Studies: The History, Representation, and Identity of China's Majority*. University of California Press, 2012.

Normore, Christina, editor. *Re-Assessing the Global Turn in Medieval Art History*. Arc Humanities Press, 2018.

Nye, Joseph. "Globalism versus Globalization: What Are the Different Spheres of Globalism – and How Are They Affected by Globalization?" *The Globalist*, April 15, 2002, www.theglobalist.com/globalism-versus-globalization/. Accessed July 9, 2020.

Pauketat, Timothy R. and Susan M. Alt. *Medieval Mississippians: The Cahokian World*. School for Advanced Research Press, 2015.

Phillips, William D. Jr. *Slavery in Medieval and Early Modern Iberia.* University of Pennsylvania Press, 2014.

Slavery from Roman Times to the Early Transatlantic Trade. University of Minnesota Press, 1985.

"Sugar Production and Trade in the Mediterranean at the Time of the Crusades." *The Meeting of Two Worlds: Cultural Exchange between East and West during the Period of the Crusades,* edited by Vladimir P. Goss and Christine Verzár Bornstein, Medieval Institute, 1986, pp. 393–406.

Redfern, Rebecca and Joseph T. Hefner. "Officially Absent but Actually Present: Bioarcheological Evidence for Population Diversity in London during the Black Death, AD 1348–50." *Bioarcheology of Marginalized People,* edited by Madeleine L. Mant and Alyson Jaagumägi Holland, Academic Press/Elsevier, 2019, pp. 69–114.

Robinson, Cedric J. *Black Marxism: The Making of the Black Radical Tradition.* 3rd ed., University of North Carolina Press, 2020.

Said, Edward. *Orientalism.* Random House, 1978.

Spivak, Gayatri Chakravorty. *Death of a Discipline.* Columbia University Press, 2003.

"How Do We Write Now?" *PMLA,* vol. 133, no. 1, 2018, pp. 166–170.

Suckale-Redlefsen, Gude. *Mauritius: Der Heilige Mohr.* Verlag Schnell & Steiner, 1987.

Thapar, Romila. *Early India: From the Origins to AD 1300.* University of California Press, 2002.

Turville-Petre, Thorlac. *England the Nation: Language, Literature, and National Identity, 1290–1340.* Clarendon Press, 1996.

Verlinden, Charles. *L'esclavage dans l'Europe médiévale I: Péninsule ibérique – France.* De Temple, 1955. Rijksuniversiteit te Gent; Werken, uitgegeven door de Faculteit van de Letteren en Wijsbegeerte vol. 119.

L'esclavage dans l'Europe médiévale II: Italie – Colonies italiennes du Levant – Levant latin, Empire byzantine. De Temple, 1977. Rijksuniversiteit te Gent; Werken, uitgegeven door de Faculteit van de Letteren en Wijsbegeerte vol. 162.

Wade, Geoff. "The Zheng He Voyages: A Reassessment." *Asia Research Institute Working Paper Series* no. 31, October 2004.

Walker, Alicia. "Globalism." *Studies in Iconography,* vol. 33, 2012, pp. 183–196.

Wallerstein, Immanuel. *The Modern World-System, Vol. I: Capitalist Agriculture and the Origins of the European World Economy in the Sixteenth Century.* Academic Press, 1974.

The Modern World-System, Vol. II: Mercantilism and the Consolidation of the European World-Economy, 1600–1750. Academic Press, 1980.

The Modern World-System, Vol. III: The Second Great Expansion of the Capitalist World-Economy, 1730–1840s. Academic Press, 1989.

"World System versus World-Systems: A Critique." *The World System: Five Hundred Years or Five Thousand?*, edited by Andre Gunder Frank and Barry K. Gills, London, Routledge, 1993, pp. 292–296.

World-Systems Analysis: An Introduction. Duke University Press, 2004.

Whitaker, Cord. *"The Invention of Race and the Status of Blackness." Cambridge Journal of Postcolonial Literary Inquiry,* forthcoming.

Wilkinson, David. "Globalizations: The First Ten, Hundred, Five Thousand and Million Years." *Globalization and Global History*, edited by Barry K. Gills and William R. Thompson, Routledge, 2006. 68–78.

Woodside, Alexander. *Lost Modernities: China, Vietnam, Korea, and the Hazards of World History.* Harvard University Press, 2006.

Yang, Shao-yun. *The Way of the Barbarians: Redrawing Ethnic Boundaries in Tang and Song China.* University of Washington Press, 2019.

Yo-Yo Ma. *The Silk Road Project*, www.silkroad.org/about. Accessed December 12, 2013.

The Global Middle Ages: An Introduction – the first title in the Cambridge University Press Elements series in the Global Middle Ages – is dedicated to Stephen G. Nichols, whose intellectual generosity, kindness, and capacious vision are of global renown.

About the Author

Geraldine Heng is Perceval Professor of Medieval Romance, Historiography, and Culture, and an affiliate of Middle Eastern Studies, Women's Studies, and Jewish Studies at the University of Texas, Austin. She is the author of *The Invention of Race in the European Middle Ages* (2018) and *England and the Jews: How Religion and Violence Created the First Racial State in the West* (2018), both published by Cambridge University Press, as well as *Empire of Magic: Medieval Romance and the Politics of Cultural Fantasy* (2003, Columbia). *The Invention of Race in the European Middle Ages* was awarded the 2019 PROSE Prize in Global History, the 2019 American Academy of Religion Prize in Historical Studies, the 2019 Robert W. Hamilton Grand Prize, and the 2020 Otto Gründler Prize. Heng is the editor of *Teaching the Global Middle Ages* (2022, Modern Language Association), coedits the University of Pennsylvania Press series, RaceB4Race: Critical Studies of the Premodern, as well as the Cambridge Elements series in the Global Middle Ages. She is currently working on a new book, Early Globalisms: The Interconnected World, 500–1500 CE. Originally from Singapore, Heng is Fellow of the Medieval Academy of America, a member of the Medievalists of Color, and Founder and Director of the Global Middle Ages Project: www .globalmiddleages.org.

Cambridge Elements ≡

The Global Middle Ages

Geraldine Heng

University of Texas at Austin

Geraldine Heng is Perceval Professor of English and Comparative Literature at the University of Texas, Austin. She is the author of *The Invention of Race in the European Middle Ages* (2018) and *England and the Jews: How Religion and Violence Created the First Racial State in the West* (2018), both published by Cambridge, as well as *Empire of Magic: Medieval Romance and the Politics of Cultural Fantasy* (2003, Columbia). She is the editor of *Teaching the Global Middle Ages* (2022, MLA), coedits the University of Pennsylvania Press series, RaceB4Race: Critical Studies of the Premodern, and is working on a new book, Early Globalisms: The Interconnected World, 500–1500 CE. Originally from Singapore, Heng is a Fellow of the Medieval Academy of America, a member of the Medievalists of Color, and Founder and Co-director, with Susan Noakes, of the Global Middle Ages Project: www .globalmiddleages.org.

Susan Noakes

University of Minnesota Twin Cities

Susan Noakes is Professor and Chair of French and Italian at the University of Minnesota Twin Cities. From 2002 to 2008 she was Director of the Center for Medieval Studies; she has also served as Director of Italian Studies, Director of the Center for Advanced Feminist Studies, and Associate Dean for Faculty in the College of Liberal Arts. Her publications include *The Comparative Perspective on Literature: Essays in Theory and Practice* (co-edited with Clayton Koelb, Cornell, 1988) and *Timely Reading: Between Exegesis and Interpretation* (Cornell, 1988), along with many articles and critical editions in several areas of French, Italian, and neo-Latin Studies. She is the Founder and Co-director, with Geraldine Heng, of the Global Middle Ages Project: www.globalmiddleages.org.

About the Series

Elements in the Global Middle Ages is a series of concise studies that introduce researchers and instructors to an uncentered, interconnected world, c. 500–1500 CE. Individual Elements focus on the globe's geographic zones, its natural and built environments, its cultures, societies, arts, technologies, peoples, ecosystems, and lifeworlds.

Cambridge Elements ≡

The Global Middle Ages

Elements in the Series

The Global Middle Ages: An Introduction
Geraldine Heng

A full series listing is available at: www.cambridge.org/EGMA

Printed in the United States
by Baker & Taylor Publisher Services